TO:
JUNE STEFANI

Capt. Anderson's
Cookbook

Best Wishes & the Patronis Family

Yonnie Patronis

by Lee Lapensohn

5551 North Lagoon Drive   Panama City Beach, Florida

Dedicated to the Memory
of
Theo J. Patronis

ISBN: 0 - 9655680 - 0 - 8

Patronis brothers Johnny (L) and Jimmy flank their father Theo.

Welcome to Capt. Anderson's

Although you may not be reading this book in the restaurant, you're still with us and the things in which we believe. We brought you this book as restaurant owners, and as a family dedicated to preserving the quality of food and service that we learned from Theo Patronis, our beloved father and grandfather.

Theo's philosophy was simple: serve people fresh, well-prepared food in a clean and wholesome environment and they will come back again and again. We do and they have.

Each season we serve so many meals that if we served them all at one time, we would be able to give two meals to every man, woman, and child in Tallahassee. And we would still have enough left over to feed every one of 50,000 fans who came to town to see Florida State win another home football game. In fact, during the month of July alone, we serve a staggering 40,000 pounds of baked potatoes.

But we're not only one of the largest restaurants of our type in the United States, we're also considered to be one of the best. Again and again we have won state and national awards for our excellence. And we appreciate them.

(Continued on page 5)

We have won the esteemed Golden Spoon Award more than a dozen times.
This annual award is presented by Florida Trend Magazine, based on independent votes
from its readers. It is considered one of the premier food awards in
the State of Florida, and coveted by those that win it once,
let alone those of us who have won it more than a dozen times.

Capt. Anderson's

Brothers Johnny (seated)
and Jimmy in 1933.

Most of all, however, we appreciate our loyal patrons. We have grown in the past thirty-plus years to an institution in the food industry of both size and excellence. And thousands of families from throughout the South return to us again and again to attest to this fact. It is for these loyal customers that we have prepared this cookbook.

We hope you will enjoy it.

Johnny Patronis

Jimmy Patronis

Theo Patronis

Yonnie Patronis

Nick Patronis

Jimmy Patronis Jr.

Kefee is as much a part of the Greek table and tradition as the wine and the olives. But kefee is not food for the stomach, it's food for the soul: it's a feeling. In fact, kefee is a benign, divine, nervous disorder of the soul. It's a fanciful, whimsical state of affairs. When you experience kefee, you're possessed by the spirit of happiness.

We at Capt. Anderson's have experienced kefee and want to share at least the term with you. Kefee inflates you without warning. It fills you with joy and then, after running its course, disappears. But the memories remain.

When we think back on our times of kefee we smile a lot. Warmly. We hope you find kefee many times over, too.

Johnny Patronis

Johnny (standing) and Jimmy with Chef Nick Patragas at Seven Seas Restaurant.

"Lose an eye but don't lose your name."

Theo J. Patronis

The history of the culinary institution known today as Capt. Anderson's Restaurant really starts on a little dot of an island in the Aegean Sea, somewhere between Greece and Turkey.

The island is called Patmos and it's one of the 12 islands that make up the archipelago called the Dodecanese.

Some might say Patmos really isn't much of a place. After all, it's only 13 square miles and it's rather sparse, with little to brag about beyond a small fishing fleet and some sun-drenched hills where the Greeks grow almonds and carobs.

Probably its single international claim to fame is that St. John wrote the Book of Revelations on Patmos. The monastery there —appropriately called "St. John Theologian" — celebrated the 900th anniversary of its founding in 1990.

But the Greek culture, so important to Patmos and the other 11 islands in the Dodecanese, remains against all odds. The Turks captured Patmos in 1453 and held it until the Italians took over in 1911. But during that period of more than 450 years the Greeks on Patmos never lost faith; never lost their language or their cultural values.

Pretty old stuff, to be sure. And pretty good stuff, too. After all, Patmos is smack in the Cradle of Civilization. It's the place where ethics and values were

(Continued on page 8)

**Theo's grandmother
Urania Poulos pictured
at 110 years of age.**

born. It's home to decades of immigrants who came to America and made America great, not the other way around.

John Patronis emigrated at turn of century

Theo J. Patronis, and his father John before him, were those immigrants. He and others from this little island out in the Aegean Sea came with the spirit that made America what she is today. Those immigrants weren't afraid of hard work and brought with them the values that we hold dear in today's all-too-busy marketplace. Family worth and individual worth. Pride of ownership. Integrity and trust. A handshake as good as a contract. A man's word is his bond.

It first started with Theo's father, John, who came to America around the turn of the 20th Century and settled initially in Apalachicola, then in Quincy near Tallahassee.

America in the early part of the 20th Century was the focus for Europeans and many of Theo's young friends and neighbors from Patmos went there. They settled in Houston, Texas, and Jackson, Mississippi. In Mobile and Montgomery, Alabama. In Apalachicola, Quincy and Tallahassee, Florida. Almost always near water. Fishing fleets were part of their heritage; in their blood.

When Theo came to America in 1913, he was a lad of 16 years with a birth date of May 8, 1897 — born in the same hundred years in which George Washington also had lived. Theo left Greece and went to Italy by boat, and then from Italy to Le Harve in France by train. He then purchased a second class ticket to America so he didn't have to go through Ellis Island, the traditional stopping off place for so many of the nation's immigrants.

Introduced oysters on half shell

Theo joined his father, John, in a

(Continued on page 9)

deli-type general store at Quincy. It had the typical round tables and a lunch counter. It was there that father and son introduced Apalachicola oysters on the half shell to Quincy customers for the first time in that small town's history. And not surprisingly so. After all, Greeks from Patmos were always close to the sea and the wonderful seafood that is known throughout the culinary world. Yes, the oysters were a hit.

Later, around 1920, Theo's younger brother Nick joined them. And for several years, Theo and Nick worked together. Not unusual unto itself until it's noted that for those same several years, they had but one joint checking account. You see, honesty and trust were merely a part of their very being.

St. John wrote the Book of Revelations on Patmos.

Before Theo first came to America, his parents had "promised" him to the daughter of another family on Patmos, as was the custom for betrothal throughout much of the Mediterranean world. He was 16 and she was only six. But when Evangleia, who had been born in Egypt, herself turned 16 years of age, Theo returned to Patmos to marry her.

What a difference in the way in which we live today. It must have been somewhat frightening for this young man to leave his island of birth, his family and friends, to come to a strange land on the other side of a great ocean.

And it must have also been at least a bit difficult for Theo to honor the wishes of his parents in his marriage to a girl of their choosing. But he was honorable. And that's the legacy that Theo got from John, and in turn gave to his own children. Theo honored his father and his mother, and he honored the culture into which he had been born.

So Theo and Evangleia established their new home in Quincy, Florida. And it is there that Johnny was born, coincidentally on the same date as his father: May 8. The year was 1928.

Shortly thereafter Theo and his young wife and son moved to Tallahassee for

(Continued on page 10)

John Patronis emigrated at turn of century; Theo followed in 1913.

greater opportunity in Florida's larger capital city. There a second son, Jimmy, was born January 19, 1931.

Beef stew 15 cents, 2 cigars for a nickel

Upon moving to Tallahassee, Theo opened the Five and Ten Cent Lunch, a restaurant which soon became popular. Close to the state capitol building, the Five and Ten, later called simply F and T, became the gathering place of governors and plumbers, legislators and lobbyists, businessmen and lawyers, college professors and civic leaders. It remained the place of choice for nearly 50 years.

Johnny has fond memories of both the restaurant and Tallahassee, which he recalls as "a wonderful

town." The Florida Legislature met there every two years and Johnny also recalls the excitement when the old legislature went into session. It always proved an opportunity for Theo's restaurant to do lots more business.

The "Five and Ten Cent Lunch" opened in 1930 and remained there until 1975.

Theo had opened during the Great Depression. Beef stew was on the menu for 15 cents, and beer was a dime. A Coca-Cola or a cup of coffee sold for five cents. You got 20 hamburgers or 20 hot dogs for a dollar. It was the type of small-town gathering place where you could get two Above The Average cigars for a nickel. With its tables and long counter, it could seat about 75. High speed torpedo ceiling fans moved Tallahassee's hot, humid summer air in swift circles; shirtsleeves were okay.

Brothers Johnny and Jimmy went to work at the restaurant as little kids. They helped Theo at the cash register, bussed tables, and in general, learned about running a successful business from their father. But it was at the cash register and the back door that they learned first.

Theo told his sons to always stay one at the cash register and the other at the back door; from there they could control the business. Johnny recalls that he and Jimmy used to fight about who would get

(Continued on page 11)

the register and who would get the back door. "We're still doing the same thing," says Johnny with a twinkle and his usual dry repartee, referring to the sharing of responsibilities at the institution now known as Capt. Anderson's.

300,000 meals
in a season

The lessons learned from Theo about cash register and back door would prepare the Patronis brothers to eventually successfully operate one of the best large-volume seafood restaurants in the United States, serving some 300,000 meals each year.

But back at the cash register in Tallahassee there was more to be learned. "Daddy was very honest, just as straight as he could be,"

Theo J. Patronis

recalls Johnny. "He would budget his time and his money. I don't know of anybody who ever questioned his honesty. He taught us how to work, not live."

But the keynote that Theo taught them, recalls Johnny, is the phrase "Lose an eye but don't lose your name." Both Johnny and Jimmy have sought to keep that phrase alive by their deeds, and Jimmy has carefully taught it to each of his four sons.

And it was at the Five and Ten that Johnny and Jimmy, young children then, first teamed together in a business venture that would start a strong business relationship that would last for more than half a century. As youngsters, they sold fireworks in front of the F & T. The building was set back so they had access to the street traffic. A good location for a temporary stand.

The next step involves Johnny, who had graduated from high school in 1946. Always the entrepreneur, he wanted to open a "modern" restaurant in Tallahassee and did so in 1947. He recalls that his dad, Theo, loaned him $3,000 to get into the business venture with George Gouras. They did so well that a second Seven Seas Restaurant was opened in Panama City in 1953. And that's how Johnny Patronis came to Bay County in the first place.

(Continued on page 12)

**Theo returned to Patmos
to marry Evangleia.**

The year 1953 also was the year that Jimmy Patronis was graduated from Florida State with a bachelor's degree in business administration. Since he was not scheduled to go into the U.S. Air Force until 1954, Jimmy helped out at the Seven Seas Restaurant until his induction. As a second lieutenant, Jimmy became a radar control officer, serving at Lakeland and Panama City in Florida and then spending 15 months in Alaska.

Responsibilities shared with next generation

When he returned from military service in October of 1955, he

bought out George Gouras' share of the Seven Seas Restaurant. So brothers Johnny and Jimmy were in business together once again, this time in a partnership that included another Greek businessman, A.J. Christo. Christo's mother, and Johnny and Jimmy's mother, had gone to school together and the families knew each other from the Old Country.

Although Christo had a controlling share of the Seven Seas, Johnny and Jimmy were the men who operated the business, and they did so along the lines of Theo's successful F & T in Tallahassee.

And the tradition has been carried on with Jimmy's sons. Yonnie started at the cash register when he was 13 and continues to oversee that function today, as comptroller of the business. And brother Jimmy Jr. helps him at the cash register. Both men have additional duties, however. Yonnie is also in charge of the bars and lounges and Jimmy Jr. is the personnel director.

Jimmy remembers with obvious pride that his son Theo "was about five years old when he started helping us clean up." And Theo has been working full-time with his dad and uncle in the business since he was graduated from high school. He's currently responsible for the major task of purchasing, a high-volume responsibility that involves such things as the purchase of 1,124,910 shrimp for a single season, 2,000 50-

(Continued on page 13)

Uncle Nick in Quincy

pound sacks of flour for a total of 100,000 pounds, 30,000 pounds of charcoal, and 38,589 souvenir glasses.

Son Nick also has been active in the business since he was old enough to count change. Today he not only assists older brother Theo as assistant purchasing agent but also oversees an intense kitchen operation, expediting a tremendous volume of prepared food: 124,989 orders of shrimp in a season; 21,737 orders of steak; 64,316 filets of grouper; 1,238 gallons of soup; 721,341 rolls, and 52,013 slices of dessert.

Johnny and Jimmy, however, have been much more than just successful restaurant owners. They also have been active supporters and participants in their community.

Good stewardship, good citizenship go together

As Johnny teaches his four nephews even today, a successful restaurant has to be a part of the community. "The more you give the more you make" remains his philosophy. "If the county does well, we do well," he says.

And Bay County responded to these two caring brothers. Civic clubs held meetings at their restaurant. The first popular Downtown Kiwanis Club pancake breakfast to raise money for children's projects began with them at the Seven Seas. And more than 30 years later, Jimmy Jr. is a member of that club, while the family still hosts various club functions.

And the Chamber of Commerce "First Friday" monthly breakfasts also started with Johnny and Jimmy Patronis at the Seven Seas, another tradition that 30 years later remains an active and productive leadership project.

But it wasn't just the roles of host in which the Patronis brothers excelled.

(Continued on page 14)

Evangleia and son Johnny

Bank of Panama City. They also were responsible for bringing the first FM radio station (WMAI) to Panama City in 1962. Both of them served on various bank boards and were involved with industrial development in the county.

Both men were supporters of environmental protection for Florida's natural resources, including, of course, advocacy for the state's fertile fishing grounds. And today the brothers and Jimmy's four sons not only run a restaurant that supports the fishing industry, they also own an important natural spring called Econfina. Econfina is one of only 75 first magnitude springs in the United States, and one of only 27 in the State of Florida. As a first magnitude spring, it pumps a minimum of 64 million gallons of water a day.

They were shirt-sleeve community leaders as well as shirt-sleeve restauranteurs.

Johnny is known to say "If you don't get a break in life, you're not going to make it." But yet he and his brother worked hard to get a break. Jimmy and his wife Helen were and remain most active in St. John the Theologian Church. Helen continues in a leadership role. Johnny was president of the Bay County Chamber of Commerce, a member of the Bay County Planning Board, and later president of the Panama City Beach Chamber of Commerce.

And together, Johnny and Jimmy owned half of the First National

Protecting a natural resource

The land surrounding the spring is protected by the Northwest Florida Water Management District. Johnny and Jimmy take great pride in this important natural resource. Water quality, they explain, is measured primarily by total dissolved solids, or TDS. The fewer the better, says Johnny. He goes on to explain that "average TDS of spring water in the United States is 190 parts per million. Econfina natural spring water is 37 parts per

(Continued on page 15)

million," he says, noting that this TDS "far exceeds all EPA and FDA standards and requirements."

The Patronis brothers hope to expand the market area for sale of this natural spring water, which went on the market in March of 1995. Their target area is the entire Southeast.

As they continued to become involved in community, regional and state-wide projects, Jimmy became a significant Florida State University football booster and Johnny became an ardent nature conservationist. Together, Johnny and Jimmy also gave scholarship support to worthy Florida State students.

Evangleia and son Jimmy

And together they donated highly-prized real estate so the county could build the Patronis Elementary School to support population growth at Panama City Beach. But the story behind the donation of the Thomas Drive site really involves Johnny's wife Opal. It was Opal who encouraged the brothers to donate the land when she learned that the county's site selection committee was unable to locate something of appropriate value.

And the Patronis brothers remain boosters of Bay County and the local economy. "We always promoted the beaches and the beaches always promoted us," says Johnny. The beaches, he says, "are the only hard-core asset that we have. From Mexico Beach to Pensacola we have the finest beaches in the United States. We must protect them," he asserts.

1967 — The founding of an institution

The critical step in the history of Capt. Anderson's Restaurant came in 1967. That's when Johnny and Jimmy Patronis bought the current location from Max and Walter Anderson.

When they left the Seven Seas after 14 years in downtown Panama City, they took the staff with them. "The strength of Capt. Anderson's is its employees," say the brothers. Their employees are like family and many of them have been with Johnny and Jimmy Patronis for 20 or more years.

(Continued on page 16)

Evangleia, Theo and Johnny at Shell Point in Wakulla County.

"I guess we treated them good," says Jimmy in obvious understatement. "They are more like family than employees. We kind of helped raise Alonzo." Jimmy Patronis is talking about Alonzo Keys, the executive chef at Captain Anderson's. Chef Keys has been with the Patronis brothers since November 8, 1953.

And there are many others. Hostess Helen "Granny" Pope has been with the brothers since July of 1968, Chris Ball at the cash register has been with them since January of 1969, server Charlene Ransburgh has been there since April of 1971, Dining Room Manager and Head Hostess Jean Brahier has been there since June, 1971, and servers Rosa Lee Davis, Carolyn Goldsberry, and Connie Torbit all started in 1972.

"We've tried to treat the employees like we've wanted to be treated," says Jimmy.

The Patronis brothers didn't just take the staff when they left downtown Panama City and moved out to Panama City Beach. They also took the customers.

"You better be prepared to marry it."

When Johnny and Jimmy bought the current location in 1967, the property spanned two acres. The restaurant had some 225 seats and included about 4,000 square feet. Max and Walter Anderson did $4,000 worth of business December of 1966. Johnny and Jimmy took over in 1967 and that December they did $16,000 worth of business. Business literally was booming.

And as business continued to grow, so did the physical capacity of the restaurant. Capt. Anderson's saw five expansions over the years to bring the physical plant to the more than 28,000 square feet it occupies

(Continued on page 17)

today, and those initial 225 seats have grown to 800.

One thing's for sure. No matter what the rate of success, one of the brothers always was on the property to supervise the preparation and service of food. A tradition that began 40 years ago in the Seven Seas Restaurant and was carried on at Capt. Anderson's Restaurant and continues even today. Johnny, Jimmy or one of the four sons always is on the property, not only to greet old and new friends, but to supervise food preparation and service.

"I think what makes a successful restaurant is the personnel. You've got to marry it, baby sit it, and watch it," says Jimmy. And Johnny agrees. "You better be prepared to marry it" if you want a successful institution like Capt. Anderson's.

Brothers Johnny (L) and Jimmy

And Jimmy speaks for his brother as well. "You need to have quality food and you need turnover so you can have fresh food. You can't work out of your freezer." And they don't. The Patronis brothers have prided themselves in serving only fresh seafood and that's been a ticket to success with the patrons and the industry alike.

Rated best in Florida over and over again

Over and over again the restaurant has captured state and regional awards for the quality of its food. More than a dozen times Florida Trend Magazine has named Capt. Anderson's recipient of the coveted Golden Spoon Award, identifying it as one of the best restaurants in the State of Florida. This has put Capt. Anderson's Restaurant in a special class, along with such others as Arthur's 27 at Lake Buena Vista, Bern's Steak House in Tampa, The Colony on Longboat Key, and Maison & Jardin, the famous French restaurant in Altamonte Springs.

(Continued on page 18)

Evangleia and Theo in Tallahassee

And in 1996, more than 3,000 readers in an independent poll tabulated at the University of Alabama for Southern Living magazine judged Capt. Anderson's their favorite seafood restaurant in the 13 Southern states, winning the Patronis brothers the impressive "Readers' Choice Award."

And as one would expect, great restaurants not only draw large crowds, they also draw patrons with special status like the late C&W star Charlie Rich, heartthrob Pat Boone, and cowboy hero Lash LaRue. Through the years there has been a long list of screen and tv actors like Mickey Gilley, Dolf Lundgren and Peter Weller. And a long list of singers such as Johnny Cash and Tanya Tucker.

Sports figures such as "Bear" Bryant, Ted Williams, Bobby Bowden and Johnny Majors were regulars. And governors, congressmen, senators and lobbyists still come to meet and eat.

Yes, Capt. Anderson's Restaurant on Grand Lagoon at Panama City Beach is an institution that would please the patriarch, Theo J. Patronis, and his father, John Patronis.

Theo always said "lose an eye but don't lose your name" and his sons and grandsons have followed that dictum.

It's a wonderful story about honest and caring men who have taken a family business and turned it into a valued institution. It's a story that proves quality remains on the American scene; that their Greek heritage has brought strength to not only their immediate family but the hundreds of employees and the thousands of patrons who come to break bread with them again and again.

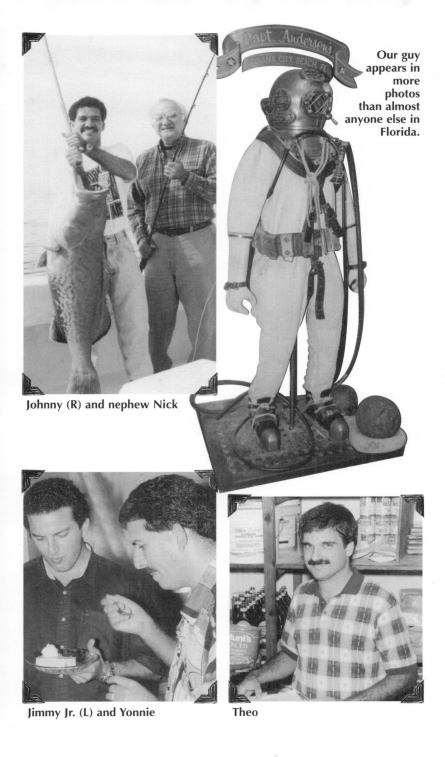

Our guy appears in more photos than almost anyone else in Florida.

Johnny (R) and nephew Nick

Jimmy Jr. (L) and Yonnie

Theo

A wonderful harvest from the Sea

There are some 20,000 species of fish in the world. In American waters alone there are hundreds.

Confusing? You bet. But that's just the half of it.

When we call a fish a redfish in the South, we're really talking about a red drum. In California, when they say redfish, it's another name for bass. And up in Long Island Sound, the fish they call porgy is the same that they call scup in Narragansett Bay.

How about those fish that change names when they change size? A lemon sole is a winter flounder or blackback when it weighs less than three and a half pounds. And scrod is merely a cod under three pounds.

Then there is the case of whitefish, a freshwater fish. That's a bit different from white fish, which is any fish with white flesh.

Enough? Well, just one last example. There is freshwater trout . . . and sea trout, a saltwater fish which is also called weakfish, related to the bass but speckled like a trout.

So there you have it. And that's part of the reason there has been so much mystery and confusion about wonderful, fresh fish. For too many years too many Americans have felt there was some sort of mystery about buying fresh fish and cooking it properly.

We hope this cookbook will take away some of that melodrama; some of that quandary. Fish, after all, is not only delicious when prepared properly, but also quite good for your health. It's the best and healthiest alternative to meat and fowl.

At Captain Anderson's Restaurant in Florida, we serve lots of fresh fish — some 300,000 meals every year. We thought you'd like to know the favorites are red snapper, grouper, tuna, pompano, scamp, flounder, and amberjack.

Second-best favorites among our dinner guests are mackerel, yellow tail, snapper, salmon, and catfish.

Because of the popularity of these fish, and the popularity of our cookbook with those who visit us for dinner, we have included some basic recipes that will work well with the fish named above.

We have also given you some tips about cooking your fish but the most important one remains this: **Do not overcook.** It's worth repeating because

(Continued on page 21)

Johnny (seated) with nephews (L-R) Yonnie, Theo, Jimmy Jr., Nick

overcooking is the one thing that so frequently steals the tenderness and taste from fish at home and in far too many restaurants.

You'll also see that we encourage you to char-broil fresh fish. Back in 1969, owner Johnny Patronis and his father Theo traveled to their native Greece to find new and exciting ways to prepare seafood. Over and over again they saw and ate fish cooked on charcoal. The Greeks have been cooking fish this way since ancient time.

When Johnny returned to Florida he put char-broiled fish on the menu at Captain Anderson's — the first restaurant in the Southeast to feature this tasty specialty . It has done nothing but grow in popularity and that's why we have included good information about this excellent method of cooking in this book.

When buying fresh fish, there are some key terms used to describe how the fish will be prepared for you. These are called "market forms" and include whole dressed, dressed, drawn, steaked, filleted, and butterflied. We use these terms at Capt. Anderson's market.

Whole fish or **round fish** means the fish is just the way it came out of the water. But if a recipe calls for a fish that is "whole," it really means one that is "whole dressed."

Whole dressed is when the fish is eviscerated and scaled, with the fins removed. Removal of the fins is routine here. But if you want it whole dressed with the backbone out so it can be stuffed, you've got to ask for it that way. Just as the backbone routinely remains, so do the head and tail.

Editor's Note: We urge you not to use the word "cleaned" when you really mean "dressed." The fish isn't dirty in the first place so it really doesn't need to be cleaned, just dressed.

(Continued on page 22)

Dressed usually means the fish is scaled and eviscerated and the head, tail and fins are removed.

When a fish is **drawn**, it means the fish is gutted through a small neck slit and therefore is not split. This works well on smaller fish with a small ventral or belly cavity. These would be fish such as smelt, herring, mackerel, or trout.

Pan dressed is similar to whole dressed, but used for smaller fish three quarters of a lb. to one and a half lbs. It means scaled, eviscerated, and usually the head, tail and fins are removed.

Steaks mean cross-section slices from large fish. They contain a piece or pieces of the backbone, which should be left in place.

Fish **fillets** also are popular. Fillets are the sides of a dressed fish cut lengthwise. In many instances the skin may be left on.

And when the two sides of a filleted fish are held together by the skin, it usually means the fish have been **butterflied.**

See, no mystery about it.

Now, how about one last word before we go into the recipes? The word involves just how much fish to buy for dinner. Here are some general rules with no particular recipe in mind.

For whole dressed fish, you ought to allow about a pound per serving, except in the case of some of the larger fish, such as red snapper. When buying fish that is pan-dressed, allow about a half pound per person. And for steaks, which have practically no waste, about a pound will serve two or three. Fillets have a rule of thumb: generally one pound serves two comfortably and three by making a filling that is a bit heavier and more filling.

Another neat formula for buying the right amount of fish for your dinner guests: ask either the teacher or the person behind the fish counter. Most stores know exactly how much you'll need, so ask.

Enjoy, enjoy.

(Continued on page 24)

Many of the pictures of our employees on task were taken by Panama City Beach photographer **Patrick Tiffany**. We appreciate his assistance in depicting the excitement and the dedication-to-excellence that is shared by our staff.

Capt. Anderson's

Johnny Patronis

Tips for Cooking Fresh Fish

Deep Fry – Heat cooking oil to 350 degrees in a fryer or deep fry pan, electric skillet, or a wok. Whole small fish or fish chunks, fingers or fillets can be deep fried. There must be enough hot cooking oil to cover the fish. Never crowd the fryer. Leave plenty of room for oil to circulate freely.

Breadings include cracker meal and flour mix, cornmeal, breadcrumbs, and flour. Dip fish in skim milk and egg mixture and then into breading. Fish is done when lightly browned about three to five minutes.

Fish should flake easily, appear opaque but remain moist. Overcooking toughens fish and detracts from flavor.

Pan Fry – Dip fish in milk (skim milk best), beaten egg, or both combined (water is satisfactory with mullet). Next dip fish, whole, chunks, fingers or fillets into breading mixture of plain flour, cracker meal and flour, cornmeal, breadcrumbs or corn flake crumbs. Heat oil in skillet and place fish in single layer into hot oil. Cook turning only once during cooking time. Check for doneness.

Bake – Place fish on oiled baking dish (pure olive oil is excellent). Bake in oven at 325 to 350 degrees until done. Fillets, steaks and whole fish are easily baked. Whole fish can be stuffed. Stuffing can be such as Pepperidge Farm with crab meat or shrimp pieces added. And all manner of mixtures can be added to fish during baking. Use lemon juice and butter generously. A rule of thumb in cooking – measure fish at thickest point. Allow ten minutes for each inch when broiling or baking.

Broil – Arrange fish in single layer on well greased broiler rack. Rack should be about four inches from heat source. Baste before, during and after broiling. Herbs, spices, tomato, butter and lemon juice make ingredients to baste fish.

Charcoal Broiled – A barbecue, charcoal or gas with grill closely spaced can be used. Generously oil both grill and fish. Coals should be hot, very hot. Fish should be placed about four inches from hot coals. Place fish on grill and halfway through cooking time, turn fish. Complete cooking and season. If grill is not spaced closely, poke several holes in a square of heavy duty aluminum foil. See our advice on page 27.

Bay leaves, fresh garlic, oregano, thyme, brand-name McIlhenny's Tabasco pepper sauce, and brand-name Lawry's Seasoning Salt. To this list add olive oil. That's because above all the other types, only the oil of olives produces the truly unique taste that our senior chefs demand. So there you have it. Our six-plus-one "must have" short list.

Capt. Anderson's

Greek Grilled Fish
(Psária Skháras Khoriátika)

1 3 1/2-lb. firm-fleshed fish,
  cleaned and scaled,
  or 4 fish steaks, at least
  1/2 inch thick
  (about 8 oz. each)
Juice of 1 lemon
  (reserve 1 juiced lemon half)

sea salt and cracked black pepper
  to taste
1/3 c. Extra-Virgin olive oil
6 sprigs of fresh oregano
3 bay leafs

There are not many culinary treats that can top fresh fish grilled over a charcoal fire and served with fresh herbs. Walk along any Greek harbor and you'll find tavérnas where the specialty is this culinary masterpiece.

For grilling, Greeks choose a variety of fish and seafood, including red mullet, bonita, tuna, swordfish, sardines, lobster, shrimp, octopus, cuttlefish, and squid.

The charcoal should be moderately hot and lightly covered with grey ash.

Herbs, both fresh and dried, are a fundamental way of flavoring grilled fish. How you use them is more important than which herbs you choose. Thyme, rosemary and oregano are favorites. We also recommend our Greek Dressing and Marinade.

The most common problems with grilled fish are drying and breaking. Guard against this by choosing plump and succulent fish of at least 1½ lbs. in weight. Smaller fish are better fried. Brush both fish and grill liberally with olive oil and take special care over cooking times. Base this on the thickness, not the length.

Dry fish with paper towels and score fish larger than 2 pounds so they cook evenly. With a sharp knife, make two or three deep 2-inch parallel diagonal incisions on each side of the fish. (The heads are always left intact on fish prepared for the grill – the cheeks taste particularly good.) Rub whole fish inside and out, steaks on both sides, with half the lemon juice, salt, pepper, and the olive oil. Dust with herbs.

Grill 4 to 5 inches above hot coals and brush with olive oil. Brush the fish with some of the remaining olive oil. Be extremely careful of flare-ups. Olive oil has a relatively low flash point. Combine the remaining lemon juice and olive oil to make a basting sauce. Grill the fish on both sides until cooked through, about 10 minutes for steaks, up to 15 minutes for smaller whole fish, and 25 minutes for larger fish.

Serve immediately.

Blackened Fish

2 tbls. seafood seasoning
(Lawry's, a pinch of thyme,
cayenne and a clove of garlic, minced)

6 tbls. butter
1/2 lb. fillets

Heat a large, seasoned cast iron skillet to a very high heat. It will take about 10 minutes. Melt the butter in a separate pan. Spread the spice mixture on a flat surface. Dip both sides of the fillets, first into the melted butter, then into the spice mixture.

Cook the fish about two minutes on each side. Check for doneness.

Grouper Marguerey

6 fillets (4 oz. each)
12-oz. can of select oysters
2 dozen medium shrimp
(raw, deveined)

2 dozen raw scallops
Mornay sauce
Parmesan cheese
coarse crumbled crackers

Bring a quantity of lightly salted water to the boiling point. Place the snapper fillets in the water and return it to the boiling point. Allow ten minutes of cooking for each inch thickness of fish. After about five minutes, add the oysters, scallops and shrimp. Cook until all four items are done.

Pour off water. Place a fillet, four oysters, four shrimp and four scallops in separate casserole dishes. Cover with Mornay sauce, a generous sprinkling of Parmesan cheese and coarse cracker crumbs. Place the dishes in a preheated 375 degree oven. Brown lightly. (Find recipe for Mornay sauce under Sauces.)

It should be noted that Florida Trend Magazine traditionally selects only a handful of restaurants throughout the state to receive the Golden Spoon award, in a state noted nationally for its many eating establishments. In order to fully appreciate the significance of the Golden Spoon Awards that have been won by us more than a dozen times, we list some of the other winners. We encourage you to patronize them for superior dining.

Arthur's 27 at Lake Buena Vista; **Bern's Steak House** in Tampa; **Chalet Suzanne** on U.S. 27 North of Lake Wales; **Chef's Garden** in Naples; **The Colony** on Longboat Key; **Maison & Jardin** in Altamonte Springs, and **Raintree** in St. Augustine.

Capt. Anderson's

Charcoal Broiled Fish
The Captain Anderson's Way

1. Whole fish or half pound fillets.

2. A very hot, very clean grill is part of the secret.

3. Grill about four inches from coals (charcoal or gas).

4. Brush fish, both sides generously with olive oil.

5. Place fish on grill. Cook, turning only once.

6. Cooking time: Rule of thumb, one-inch thickness, ten minutes total. (Half of time on each side.)

7. Check for doneness with fork (push aside skin and meat – fish should flake and meat should be opaque, but still moist).

8. With skinned fish push aside meat and check as above.

9. Fish with skin have less tendency to stick.

10. Do not salt skinned fish before cooking. It will make the surface hard. (Salt is anhydrous and pulls moisture out.)

11. Season fish when done, with salt, pepper, lemon, seafood seasoning if desired, chopped parsley and chopped green onion tops, drizzle olive oil, melted butter or margarine over fish and serve.

12. Do not overcook.

13. Do not overcook.

14. Do not overcook.

15. Do not overcook.

Fish stock is the culinary cornerstone of France's redoubtable bisques, bouillabaisses, bourrides, cotriades, matelotes, and pauchauses. Fish stock is equally important in the caldeiradas of Portugal, the paellas of Spain, the zuppa di pesces of Italy, the waterzoois of Belgium, the vis filets met kaas saus of the Netherlands, the grune krabbensuppe of Germany, the chlodnik z ryby of Poland, the solynakas and ukhas of Russia, the gelfite fish of Lithuania, and the fiskegratengs and fiskesuppes of Scandinavia.

Capt. Anderson's

**Mike Smith,
with us since
February, 1986.**

Carolina Shrimp Pie

1 c. of raw rice
5 tbls. tomato ketchup
2 cups water
2 1/2 tbls. Worcestershire
1 tsp. salt
salt and pepper to taste
1/4 c. butter
2 lbs. shrimp
2 eggs
1 c. milk
pinch of mace

Cook rice in salted water until very soft; stir in butter. Combine ingredients with cooked shrimp, adding enough milk to make mixture the consistency of a thick custard. Put in buttered casserole and bake in moderate oven 30 minutes or until brown on top. Serves 8.

Shrimp Scampi

2 pounds large shrimp
  (peeled, deveined with tails)
2 sticks unsalted butter
1/2 cup olive oil
1/4 cup fresh chopped parsley

4 cloves of garlic (crushed)
1/2 teaspoon salt
dash of cayenne pepper
1/4 cup lemon juice
2 tablespoons white wine

Melt butter, pour into a small baking dish. Add olive oil, 4 or 5 tablespoons of parsley, the garlic, salt, cayenne and lemon juice. Mix to blend well and add the shrimp, mixing to coat the shrimp evenly. Refrigerate to marinate for an hour or so.

Next arrange the shrimp in a single layer in a large skillet on medium heat, sauté the shrimp for about five minutes. Turn shrimp and sauté other side of shrimp for about five minutes longer, or until shrimp are a pretty pink.

Remove shrimp from skillet, place on a heated platter and pour the garlic mixture over them. Sprinkle with rest of parsley and garnish with lemon slices.

Tyrone Sly has been with us since March, 1977.

Nell Smith (L), with us since February, 1973.

Arthur Hooks (below), with us since May, 1990.

Stuffed Flounder

10 or 12 flounder fillets	3 tbls. lemon juice
3 tbls. chopped parsley	4 tbls. melted butter

Mix the melted butter, parsley and lemon juice to use as a dressing for the flounder fillets after cooking.

Place one half of the flounder fillets on the bottom of a baking dish. Pile crab meat stuffing on top of each fillet and add a fillet on top. Then spoon a quantity of the stuffing on the top fillets.

Make a slit in the top fillet, making sure to cut through the bottom fillet. Bake in a 350 degree preheated oven for about twenty-five minutes. Check for doneness. Stuffing should be hot all the way through and fish should flake and be opaque, but still be moist.

Drizzle the parsley and butter mixture juice over the top.

You may use whole fish, flounder, snapper or trout (almost any fish can be stuffed). Simply fill or partly fill the cavity with the stuffing. Other than crab meat stuffing can be used.

We thought you'd like to know our patrons' favorite finfish are red snapper, grouper, tuna, pompano, scamp, flounder, and amberjack

Capt. Anderson's

Famous Crab Meat Stuffing

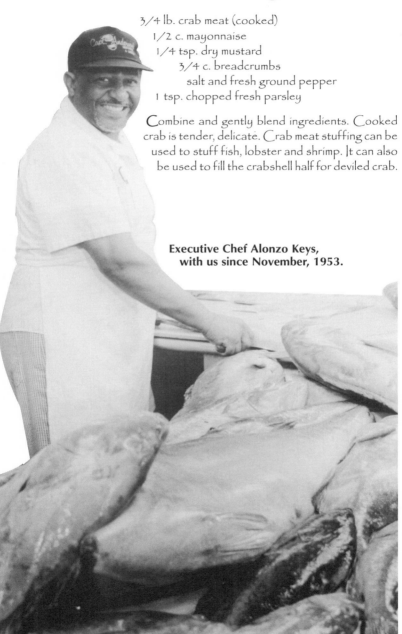

3/4 lb. crab meat (cooked)
1/2 c. mayonnaise
1/4 tsp. dry mustard
3/4 c. breadcrumbs
salt and fresh ground pepper
1 tsp. chopped fresh parsley

Combine and gently blend ingredients. Cooked crab is tender, delicate. Crab meat stuffing can be used to stuff fish, lobster and shrimp. It can also be used to fill the crabshell half for deviled crab.

**Executive Chef Alonzo Keys,
with us since November, 1953.**

Baked Fish with Tomatoes
(Psari Plakie)

1/2 c. olive oil	1/2 c. white wine
2 large onions, chopped	dash of salt
1 16-oz. can tomatoes	pepper
1 garlic clove, pressed	3 lbs. fish fillets
1/2 c. chopped fresh parsley	(grouper, snapper or bass)

Heat olive oil in saucepan, add onions and cook until translucent. Add tomatoes, wine, parsley, salt and pepper. Simmer, covered for about 10 minutes.

In last five minutes add fresh garlic. Place fish in baking dish. Cover with sauce and bake at 350 degrees for about twenty-five minutes. Fish should easily flake, but remain moist.

Baked Snapper
(Plakie)

1 3/4 lbs. filet snapper	3 medium tomatoes, chopped
salt and pepper	2 ribs celery, chopped
1/2 c. oil	2 cloves fresh garlic
1 large onion, sliced	juice of 1/2 lemon
5 new potatoes sliced	

Wash filets. Rub lemon juice on fish. Salt and pepper. Sauté onion in oil. When onion is translucent, add tomatoes, garlic and celery. Simmer over low heat. Add potatoes and simmer for about ten more minutes. Lightly oil a baking pan. Place fish in the pan and pour the tomato-potato mixture over the fish. Add 1/2 cup of water and cover with aluminum foil. Bake at 350 for one hour.

Oregano is on our "must have" list. The best oregano comes from Greece. It is stronger and sharper than the Italian. The word oregano is from the Greek, meaning "joy of the mountains." That's because it covers the hills and mountain slopes and perfumes the air. We think it should be "joy of the kitchen" and you should cover your hills and mountains of food with it. Oregano does exceptionally good things to many fish dishes. But again, fresh is best and whole leaf second to that. Enjoy.

Capt. Anderson's

Shellfish, Mollusks, and Bivalves

There are about a dozen types of shellfish eaten in the United States. Although some are more popular than others, it often is not because of a matter of taste but because of regional availability. Shellfish always should be as fresh as possible; hence, regional popularity.

The basic types are abalone, clams, crabs, crayfish, frogs' legs, lobster, oysters, mussels, scallops, shrimps, and snails.

Clams are a bivalve mollusk with a small amount of meat and a wonderful, delicate flavor. The four popular types are quahogs, steamers, skimmers, and geoducks (pronounced gooey duck). Quahogs are found along the Atlantic Coast and have a strong taste, so they are used in chowders or eaten raw. "Cherrystone" and "littleneck" are market designations, indicating size, the littleneck being the smaller. Any quahog larger than 3 inches in diameter is called a "chowder clam."

The soft shell clams popularly known as steamers are best when they come from the Chesapeake Bay. Third all along the Atlantic Coast is the surf clam or skimmer or "bar clam." It is the most widely used, especially canned. On the Pacific Coast, the geoduck is popular, along with razor clams and butter clams.

Crabs, those wonderful crustaceans with the sweet, delicate meat, rank with lobster and shrimp as an ultimate gift from the sea. There are two types of Atlantic blue crabs: hard shell and soft shell. The hard shells are found all along the Atlantic Coast. Males are called "Jimmies" and females are called "sooks." Soft-shell crabs are blues that have molted, or shed their shells. The dungeness crab is found along the West Coast, from Alaska to Southern California. Southern or Florida Stone Crabs are obviously found in those areas. It is a hard-shell variety and unlike the Atlantic blue or the Pacific dungeness, only the claws are eaten.

Mussels, those bivalve mollusks similar to clams and oysters, are enjoyed steamed, baked, or in chowders. Clinging to rocks along both East and West coasts, the blue mussel is one of the most delicious and neglected of all our seafoods. Along with lobsters, Maine produces the best mussels. They are distinguished by the vertical grain on the shell, while others have more horizontal lines.

(Continued on page 34)

The protein content of those bivalve mollusks that we call mussels is about the same as a good steak. But steak has four times as many calories and 18 times more fat.

Capt. Anderson's

Oysters have a gray-white, tender meat. These popular bivalve mollusks are prized raw in the half shell, in soups, fried, or broiled. They have been a gourmet's delight since ancient time. The ancient Greeks served them at banquets and the Romans imported them all the way from Britain packed in snow. American Indians ate oysters long before white men set foot on the Continent, and the early colonists quickly learned to enjoy oysters too. The three species of American oysters are Eastern or native, Olympia, and Western or Pacific. While western oysters are graded by size, eastern oysters are graded by name. Eastern oysters often are sold live and in the shell, by dozen or pint or quart. A quart averages 36 medium oysters.

Oysters are among Florida's products of the sea in which great pride is taken. Apalachicola is famous for better-quality oysters. Oystering has been the chief occupation there for both harvesting and shucking. Apalachicola is also the site of a one-time great cotton exchange and barge-commerce center. With its many antique shops and restored architecture it is a charming place to visit.

Scallops lack the siphons of most similar bivalves. It therefore swims by compressing its shell valves open and shut, forcing the water backwards in jets and itself forward. This movement develops a muscle called the "eye" which is the part that we eat in America. In Europe, the entire scallop, including the mass that surrounds the muscle, is eaten. Because scallops cannot close their shells tightly and lose body moisture quickly, they die soon after being removed from the water. So it is customary to shuck them at sea aboard the fishing boats and sell them raw but not in their shells.

Legend has it that St. James, the first of Jesus' disciples to become a martyr, was closely associated with scallops as a religious symbol. Buried in Spain, James is said to have risen again in 844 to lead the Christians in battle and victory against the Moors. In the 12th Century, a cathedral was built in his honor in the village of Compostela. Pilgrims to Santiago de Compostela were given a scallop shell to signify having completed the journey. A number of pilgrims were French and they identified St. James with the scallop, hence the French name for scallop which is Coquille Saint-Jacques.

(Continued on page 35)

Lobsters are the most coveted of America's shellfish, even if shrimp are by far the most popular. These wonderful crustaceans with their mottled green shells are so prized today that it's hard to believe they were mere plentiful food for the poor in Colonial days. Most often, the colder the water the sweeter the lobster meat. That's why sumptuous Maine lobsters are prized above others caught along the East coast.

Capt. Anderson's

Shrimp, the most popular shellfish of all

Shrimp, the most popular crustacean of all, is an ancient Greek delicacy. Shrimp are sold according to count and the size may also determine the market price. The very largest size sometimes is called a prawn, and in Great Britain, no matter what the size, shrimp are called prawns. (Actually, a prawn is a crayfish.)

In Eastern markets, the following rules usually apply:

Colossal 10 and under = 1 lb.
Jumbo 10-15 = 1 lb.
Large 16-20 = 1 lb.
Medium 21 to 30 = 1 lb.
Small 31 to 35 = 1 lb.
Tiny ocean shrimp 150 to 180 = 1 lb.
(These are only sold shelled and cooked.)

For your information, one pound of raw shrimp will yield on the average 1/2 to 3/4 pounds of cooked, shelled meat. Keep in mind that a half pound per person might be a good rule of thumb for a main course.

Snails include periwinkle, winkle, and conch. (Please see conch.)

Squid and Octopus often are thought of as fish but actually, they are not fish at all but mollusks. The ancient Greeks named them cephalopods because the feet (podos) grew out of the head (kephale). They are the most highly evolved of all the mollusks, being the only ones to have a centralized nervous system.

Squid and octopus are popular in many cuisines throughout the world, but curry less favor with Americans. Squid is caught along the East Coast from the Carolinas to New England and the Atlantic long-finned squid is found from Nova Scotia to Florida. Recipes for squid and octopus may be found on page 62.

Peeling Shrimp

Peeling shrimp either "green" or boiled is not a difficult procedure. Use the

(Continued on page 36)

Crayfish are lobster-like crustaceans, but without claws. Also called crawfish or "crawdads," these small crustaceans can be found all the way from the bayous of Louisiana to the creeks around Lake Michigan; from New York and Connecticut all the way to the Pacific Northwest. Often ignored in great part in all but Louisiana, the French make a big fuss about them, and they are consumed in great quantity as just about national treasures by the Fins and the Swedes.

Capt. Anderson's

thumbnail to begin to remove the shell and with the side of the thumb push back the rest of the shell.

To devein, use a paring knife with the tip slightly bent. Hold the shrimp between the thumb and forefinger and cut part way through the back and at the same time remove the sand vein. With practice you can become quite rapid. The sand vein is often removed when the head is pinched off. Many people demand that the vein be removed if only for cosmetic reasons.

A dozen or so boiled shrimp with a red sauce with a bit of character is gourmet eating. For the red sauce, take 1/2 cup of ketchup and a spoonful of prepared horseradish, add two or three drops of Tabasco and a dash or two of lemon juice. Blend and it's ready.

Boiled Shrimp

Boiling shrimp is not much different than boiling potatoes, but because of the difference in price more attention should be paid to the process.

First take a quantity of headed, unpeeled green shrimp. Bring a quantity of water to boil (sufficient to cover the shrimp). Add a small amount of salt. Adding other spices such as shrimp boil is not recommended. Shrimp are of delicate flavor, don't diminish it or cover it up.

After water has come to the second boil, boil for five to seven minutes and test one for doneness. Do not overcook. The finished shrimp should retain a texture and should not be soft and soggy.

If shrimp are done remove from heat and drain. If they need a little more cooking turn off heat and let remain in water for a little time. Check again for doneness. Drain and run cold water over them.

Broiled Shrimp

12 large shrimp, peeled and deveined	1/2 c. olive oil
clove garlic, chopped fine	sprinkle of salt
1 tbl. chopped parsley	fresh ground pepper
	3 tbls. lemon juice

Marinate shrimp in mixture listed for a few hours. Place single layer of shrimp in broiling pan and marinate. Broil 7 to 8 minutes, turning once. Do not overcook.

For preparation of the chowders of New England, the cioppinos of California, and the gumbos and court bouillons of Southern Louisiana, fish stock is indispensable.

Capt. Anderson's

Fried Shrimp

2 lbs. raw shrimp	1 c. of cracker meal
3 egg whites	1/4 c. plain flour
1/2 c. skim milk	salt and pepper

Place one layer deep on flat pan, with added layers separated by wax paper. Refrigerate for an hour or more.

When ready to cook heat fat to 325 or 350 degrees. Use deep fat thermometer to check. Cook about three or four minutes until golden brown. Drain and serve hot. Do not overcook.

- Egg white rather than whole egg will allow shrimp to cook a lighter color.

- For deep frying use a large wok with oil a couple inches deep. Cook a few at a time. You can use an electric skillet with about two inches of good quality liquid shortening.

- Pre-breading allows the breading to adhere to the shrimp. You will get a better finished product.

- When you devein a shrimp for deep frying, press your thumb along the body of the shrimp. A butterfly shrimp results. They cook quicker than a round shrimp and look larger.

- By the way, a green or uncooked whole shrimp will lose about half its weight when headed, peeled and deveined.

Fried shrimp, red or tartar sauce, a baked potato with unsalted butter and sour cream, fresh chopped green onion tops, a tomato Greek salad and a pair or more of light and onion flavored hush puppies makes a gourmet dinner.

Bouquet Garni is the traditional culinary posy, or nosegay. It has three common aromatic herbs, generally tied in a bundle or in a cheesecloth sack. They are parsley, thyme, and bay leaves. Many chefs add the bundle to sauces, casseroles, stews, and soups, removing it before serving. The proportions of the three main ingredients change according to the dish involved. In special cases, a bouquet garni may contain rosemary or lemon thyme or tarragon.

Capt. Anderson's

Stuffed Shrimp

Peel and devein a pound to a pound and a half of 16-20 count. Cut shrimp along back, being careful not to cut all the way through. Fill with crab meat stuffing, packing firmly. Brush with olive oil. Bake at 375 for about 10 minutes.

Shrimp may also be broiled for about five minutes on each side. Stuffing recipe on page 31.

Broiled Scallops and Peppers

1 quart bay or sea scallops
1/2 tsp. salt
1 tsp. paprika
1 garlic clove, crushed
cream sherry
1/4 c. Virgin olive oil

1/2 c. chopped onion
1/2 c. green peppers,
  chopped fine
1/2 c.
1 oz. capers

Put scallops in a baking dish. Combine other ingredients. Broil, stirring occasionally, until scallops are a light golden brown. Be careful not to overcook. Serve with toast points.

Fried Scallops

white of three eggs
skim milk

cracker meal
  mixed with 20 percent flour

In an electric skillet, wok or other pan, heat cooking oil to 350. Check with deep fat thermometer. Dry scallops and dip in egg white mixed with small amount of water. Then dip into cracker meal mixture. Coat evenly. Cook for three minutes and check for doneness. Scallops are extra tender. Little cooking is required, only enough to reach a golden hue. Do not overcook; they can become rough and tasteless.

Greek cuisine is a relatively simple one. Unlike the French or the Chinese or the Italians, who turn to so many sauces to expand their culinary bag of tricks, the Greek chef does just fine with a healthy portion of olive oil, a splash or so of red wine vinegar or fresh lemon juice, and a handful of cloves of fresh garlic.

Capt. Anderson's

Lobster Newburg

3 c. diced raw lobster	1/2 c. dry sherry
4 tbls. butter	1 tsp. paprika
1 1/2 c. cream	1 tbl. cognac
4 egg yolks	(optional)

Melt butter in a large skillet, add the lobster meat and sauté until the lobster turns pink. Sprinkle with paprika. Add the sherry and cook until wine is almost cooked away. Add the sweet cream blended with the eggs, well-beaten. Stir gently until the sauce is thickened. Add the cognac if desired. Spoon into individual casserole dishes and sprinkle with paprika. Serve hot.

Lobster Thermidor

4 c. cubed lobster	1/2 c. dry white wine
3 tbls. butter	1 tsp. prepared mustard
3 shallots (green onions)	1 tsp. chopped parsley
chopped	1 1/2 c. Mornay sauce

Melt butter in a skillet, add lobster meat and sauté until lightly browned. Add chopped onions and the dry white wine. Cook until volume of wine is reduced. Add the mustard, the chopped parsley and blend in the Mornay sauce. Spoon into a casserole dish or individual casserole dishes. Spread a little Mornay sauce over the tops, sprinkle with Parmesan cheese and brown under the broiler. Mornay sauce recipe is on page 57.

Greek cuisine boasts what food writer Diane Kochilas calls "an unabiding loyalty to the seasons — a faithful and stubborn insistence that everything be fresh and 'in its time' — and a reliance on the simplest, purest foods straight from nature. Olives and olive oil, honey, grapes, and a handful of herbs, spices, and nuts are so tied to the culture, so ancient in their uses and consumption, that Greek food just would not be the same without them." Basic. Fresh. Seasonal. That's exactly the philosophy that has helped make our restaurant an institution of national renown.

Capt. Anderson's

Fettucine Alfredo
with Shrimp and Crab Meat

1 lb. fettuccine boiled and strained	4 oz. Parmesan cheese
1/4 lb. butter clarified	1-lb. shrimp, boiled and cleaned
4 cloves garlic, minced	1/2 lb. lump crab meat,
salt and pepper to taste	cartilage removed
1 quart heavy whipping cream or	1/2 c. chopped parsley
Half and Half	

In saucepan, sauté garlic and butter lightly. Do not burn. Stir in whipping cream, reduce heat to low and continue stirring about 2 minutes. Add Parmesan cheese, stirring in about 1 minute. Arrange shrimp and crab meat over fettuccini and top with Alfredo Sauce. Garnish with chopped parsley. Serves 6.

Roast Leg of Lamb
(Psito Arni)

8 to 10lb. leg of lamb	fresh garlic
juice of 1 lemon	oregano
salt and pepper	rosemary
1/4 lb. butter	

Rub the leg of lamb generously with lemon juice. In a small pan mix together butter, salt, pepper, some minced garlic and oregano and rosemary. Make several deep slits in the lamb and push a sliver of garlic into each. Add 1 cup of water to baking pan. Bake at 375 degrees for 2 3/4 hours until done. During cooking brush lamb several times with the butter and herb mixture.

With typical good humor, celebrated author and television cook Jeff Smith says "Buy a bottle of retsina, a pound of Greek olives, some feta cheese, and you have one of the oldest take-out lunches in the world. He also points out that "we are indebted to Greece for the frying pan, the bain-marie (double boiler), and bechamel sauce (white sauce)."

Capt. Anderson's

Award-Winning Angel of Venice

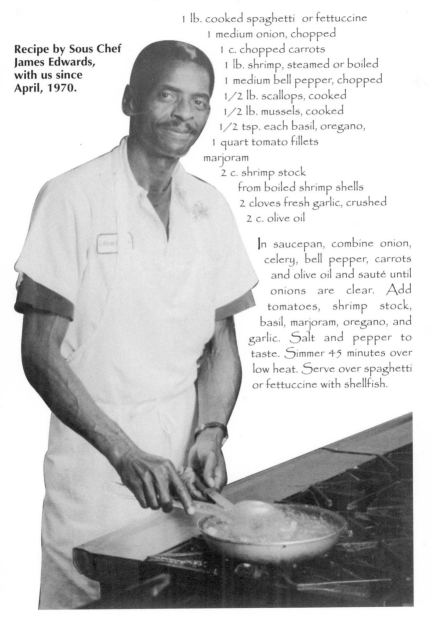

Recipe by Sous Chef James Edwards, with us since April, 1970.

1 lb. cooked spaghetti or fettuccine
1 medium onion, chopped
1 c. chopped carrots
1 lb. shrimp, steamed or boiled
1 medium bell pepper, chopped
1/2 lb. scallops, cooked
1/2 lb. mussels, cooked
1/2 tsp. each basil, oregano,
1 quart tomato fillets
marjoram
2 c. shrimp stock
from boiled shrimp shells
2 cloves fresh garlic, crushed
2 c. olive oil

In saucepan, combine onion, celery, bell pepper, carrots and olive oil and sauté until onions are clear. Add tomatoes, shrimp stock, basil, marjoram, oregano, and garlic. Salt and pepper to taste. Simmer 45 minutes over low heat. Serve over spaghetti or fettuccine with shellfish.

Rice-Stuffed Grape Leaves
(Dolmadakia Yialantzi)

1 jar (16 ozs.) grape leaves, or
   1/2 lb. fresh leaves
1/4 c. plus 2 tbls. olive oil
1 medium red onion, finely chopped
   (about 1/2 c.)
1/2 c. chopped scallions
1 c. long-grain rice
2 garlic cloves, finely chopped
1 tsp. ground cumin
1/4 c. plus 2 tbls. finely
   chopped fresh fennel

1/2 c. finely chopped fresh dill
1/2 c. finely chopped fresh
   parsley
11/2 tsps. dried mint
Salt and freshly ground pepper,
   to taste
4 to 5 c. water
strained fresh juice of 2 lemons
plain yogurt (optional)

Rinse grape leaves well to rid them of briny taste. Bring enough water to cover grape leaves amply to a rolling boil, and drop the leaves in for 3 to 5 minutes to soften – whether using fresh or preserved. Remove and drain very well in a colander. Set aside to cool.

In a large heavy skillet, heat 2 tablespoons of olive oil. Sauté onion and scallions until translucent. Add rice and sauté until very lightly browned, 3 to 5 minutes, stirring frequently. Lower heat. Add garlic, cumin, salt, pepper, and 2 cups of water. Cover and simmer until rice is softened but not cooked and liquid has been absorbed. Remove skillet from heat and let cool. When the mixture is completely cooled, mix in fennel, dill, parsley, and mint, as well as 2 tablespoons olive oil or 1 raw egg, to keep rice moist while cooking.

Spread 1 to 2 tablespoons olive oil plus 3 tablespoons water on bottom of a heavy soup pot. Sort the grape leaves and spread torn or unusable ones on bottom of pot, enough to cover the surface. Snip any hard stems from all the leaves before using.

Taking about 1 teaspoonful at a time, place rice filling at center of leaf. First fold up the bottom portion of leaf, then the left then right edges, and roll

(Continued on page 43)

Greek wine dates as far back as 5000 B.C., when grape vines were introduced from Asia. The Greeks then spread the vine throughout the ancient world and the famous wines of Jerez, Malaga, Sicily, and Germany's Rhone Valley can trace their vineyards directly to the Greeks.

Capt. Anderson's

Shrimp-Crab Au Gratin

1 lb. small cooked shrimp
1 lb. cooked crab meat
6 oz. medium cheddar cheese
Parmesan cheese
2 tbls. butter
6 tbls. plain flour
basic cream sauce

2 tbls. dry chablis
unsalted butter
cracker crumbs
1/2 c. whole milk
1 c. Half and Half
white pepper and salt

Melt butter and stir in flour to blend. Add milk and Half and Half and gently cook, stirring constantly until well blended. Do not boil. (This is a basic cream sauce or white sauce.) To a buttered casserole, add shrimp and crab. Pour sauce over the seafood and add cheese.

Sprinkle Parmesan cheese and cracker crumbs over the dish. Dot with butter and brown at 375.

(Continued from page 42)

upward to close. Place 1 dolmada at a time, seamside down, on bottom of pot. Continue until all the filling is used. Sprinkle lemon juice over grape leaves. Add about 2 cups of water. Place a plate directly on top of dolmades to keep them from opening, and then cover pot with lid. Place over medium heat and bring liquid to a boil. Reduce heat to low and simmer, covered, for at least 2 hours, until rice is cooked and grape leaves tender. Serve warm or cold, alone, with yogurt, or with béchamel. Yield: About 5 dozen.

Although Greek culture and heritage so heavily include wine, the real national drink today is ouzo. This is a clear and unctuous licorice-flavored liqueur distilled from the residuals of the grapes, after they have been pressed for wine. Ouzo was developed toward the end of the Century and no contemporary Greek dinner is complete without it.

Capt. Anderson's

Baked Spaghetti
(Pastitsio)

1 lb. large elbow macaroni	small can tomato paste
2 1/2 lbs. ground beef	plus one can of water
1 onion, chopped	1 tsp. sugar
3 cloves garlic, chopped	salt to taste
dashes of oregano, basil	2/3 c. grated Parmesan
and cinnamon	

Sauté meat with onions until juices are absorbed. Add remaining ingredients and simmer for 20 minutes. Cook macaroni in lightly salted water to al dente.

For a Cream Sauce

1 1/2 sticks of butter	6 eggs
1 1/2 c. plain flour	2 c. grated Parmesan
2 quarts milk	or Romano cheese
salt and pepper to taste	

Melt the butter and stir in the flour until thickened. Slowly add milk and mix. Remove from heat and add eggs, one at a time, then add two thirds of the cheese. To the drained macaroni add another two thirds of the cheese and stir well. Add part of the cream sauce to the macaroni so that it is well coated.

Spread two thirds of the macaroni and cream sauce mixture in a baking dish about 15 x 10 x 2. Sprinkle with cheese, add the meat sauce and sprinkle more cheese. Add remaining macaroni, cover with cream sauce and sprinkle with remaining cheese. Put a little paprika over the top. Bake at 350 for 45 minutes.

Any cream sauce left may be refrigerated or frozen for future use. Pastitsio keeps well, frozen.

The better chefs from all cultures, especially those where wine is so important such as France, Italy, Germany and, of course, Greece, quickly will tell you there is a stunning difference in flavor between good quality and poor quality vinegar. For salad dressings, we encourage you to use only a good quality, red-wine vinegar.

Capt. Anderson's

Jumbo Lump Meat Crab Cakes

1 lb. crab meat	1 tbl. parsley, chopped
1/2 c. breadcrumbs	2 tsps. Worcestershire
(or cracker crumbs)	1 tsp. prepared mustard
1 egg lightly beaten	1/2 tsp. salt
4 tbls. mayonnaise	1/2 tsp. pepper

Remove cartilage from crab meat. Mix breadcrumbs or coarse cracker crumbs with mayonnaise, egg, parsley, Worcestershire sauce, mustard, pepper and salt. Add crab meat to mixture and fold thoroughly (be gentle). Form into six cakes.

Deep fat fry or pan fry in a small amount of shortening. Deep fry at 350 degrees. Pan fry about five minutes on each side.

Sautéed Soft Shell Crab with Crab Meat

12 jumbo soft shell crabs cleaned	1/2 c. clarified butter or
1 lb. lump crab meat,	margarine
cartilage removed	1 tbl. apple cider
salt and pepper to taste	vinegar
1 c. flour, all purpose	

Heat margarine until hot. Dust soft shell crab with flour Sauté crab until golden brown on one side about 3 minutes, turn and repeat. Salt and pepper to taste. In separate sauté pan, add butter or margarine, heat and add crab meat. Sauté until hot, add salt and pepper and apple cider vinegar. Top soft shells with crab meat and serve immediately. Serves 6.

Quatre Epices is the classic French spice mix. It is used on just about everything but desserts. This recipe makes 1 1/2 cups. Give it a try. We think you'll like it.
1 c. ground white pepper; 4 tbl. freshly grated nutmeg; 3 1/2 tbl. powdered ginger; 1 1/2 tbl. powdered cloves

Capt. Anderson's

Thousand Island Dressing

2 tbls. chili sauce
1/2 tbl. vinegar
1/2 tbl. chopped green peppers
1/2 tsp. paprika

1/2 tbl. ketchup
1/2 tbl. chives
1/2 tbl. chopped pimentos

Mix well and serve. Yield: about 1 cup.

Bleu Cheese Dressing

3/4 lb. Bleu Cheese
1/2 c. French dressing
1 tbl. lemon juice
white pepper to taste
3/4 tsp. sugar

1 1/2 c. mayonnaise
1 clove garlic, minced
3 tsp. dry mustard
1 tsp. Worcestershire sauce

Blend ingredients well with a half lb. of the cheese. Reserve rest. Allow to stand at least 12 hours to mellow. Just prior to serving, add a quarter pound of Bleu Cheese crumbled coarsely. Yield: 1 pint.

French Dressing

1 small onion, sliced
3/4 tsp. salt
1/4 tsp. paprika
3/4 c. olive oil

1/4 c. vinegar or lemon juice
1/8 tsp. pepper
1 tbl. sugar

Add onion to vinegar, let stand 20 minutes; strain. If you want a stronger dressing, you can use a clove of garlic instead of the onion. Combine salt, pepper, paprika and sugar in jar or large bottle. Add vinegar and oil, cover closely and shake vigorously. French dressing may be made in larger amounts and refrigerated. Always shake or beat again before serving. Yield: about 1 cup.

The proportion of oil to vinegar in a salad dressing is approximately 4 of oil to 1 of vinegar. Pure or virgin olive oil is best. Vinegar supplies tartness and adds piquancy. A poor one will destroy natural food flavors. Good cider or wine vinegar is best.

Capt. Anderson's

Famous Greek Dressing and Wonderful Marinade

2 tbls. Lawry's
  seasoned salt
1 tsp. fresh ground pepper
2 cloves fresh garlic, minced

1 tbl. oregano
1 tbl. Hungarian paprika
4 oz. wine vinegar

Place above ingredients in a quart jar with two ounces of water and shake well. Add four ounces of wine vinegar. Fill jar within an inch of the top with Virgin or Extra Virgin olive oil. Shake well to blend and always shake before using. This dressing is so good we use it all the time, for salads and as a marinade for our fresh fish and chicken. And Lawry's seasoned salt is the ideal mixture. Captain Anderson's purchases product in fifty-pound pails, several at a time.

Greek Garlic Sauce
(Skordalia)

6 slices dry bread
  crusts trimmed off
1 medium boiled potato
12 cloves garlic, peeled
1/2 tsp. salt

1/4 tsp. fresh ground pepper
2 1/2 c. olive or salad oil
1 1/2 c. white vinegar
3 large egg yolks

Put bread, boiled potato, garlic, salt and pepper in blender. Mix well, alternating first oil, then vinegar. Lastly add egg yolks and mix three or four minutes until well blended.

There are two main types of salad dressings: warm and cold. The uncooked includes simple oil and acid mixtures like French dressing, mayonnaise and modifications of the two. The other, cooked dressings, are usually thickened with egg or flour or some ingredient that acts as a permanent binder.

Capt. Anderson's

Fish Velouté
(Velouté de Poisson)

2 tbls. butter	1 c. hot fish stock
2 tbls. flour	sea salt, freshly ground pepper

In a heavy saucepan, melt the butter, then stir in the flour with a wooden spoon. Cook over low heat for one minute, stirring constantly. The mixture should have no more than a yellowish tan color. Remove pan from fire and after the mixture stops bubbling, pour in the hot, but not boiling, fish stock all at once, whisking as you do. Return to a moderate heat, bring to a slow boil, whisking constantly, then let simmer for 10 minutes. Makes a cup.

Editor's Note: If you are not going to use the sauce immediately, film the surface with a tablespoon of stock so a skin does not form. If the velouté is to be served plain, and not used as the base of a more complicated sauce, it is usually enriched with a liaison of cream and egg yolks. Bring 2 cups of velouté sauce to a boil, reduce until it reaches the consistency of light cream and is reduced by about half.

In a small bowl, beat together 3 egg yolks and 1 cup of heavy cream. Season with a pinch of crushed pepper and one of grated nutmeg. Add a little bit of the warm sauce to the egg mixture, then pour the mixture into the remainder of the sauce, whisking constantly. Return the sauce to the stove and heat gently, whisking continuously, but do not let the sauce boil. Remove from heat and stir until cooled. Makes about 2 cups. When velouté is enriched in this way it is sometimes called Sauce Parisienne.

The famous Greek cheese, feta, is white and crumbly with a slightly sour, salty flavor. It is moderately priced. Feta means "slice" and the name is given because of the way in which large blocks are cut. Traditional feta is pickled or salted. Rennin, an enzyme, is added to the fresh milk to start the pickling process. A good feta has a flaky texture and a mildly salty, fresh flavor. Real feta is best eaten young, which means ripened for a month or two.

Capt. Anderson's

Fish Stock

2 lbs. fish bones and heads
1 stalk celery with leaves, coarsely chopped
1 onion, peeled and coarsely chopped
1 clove garlic, unpeeled and flattened with a knife
1/4 tsp. dried thyme
1 bay leaf
10 black peppercorns
5 sprigs parsley
1 leek stalk (just white part), well washed and coarsely chopped
salt and pepper to taste
1 c. dry white wine

This may be used instead of water or clam broth in fish soups. Cover with water, bring to rolling boil, then simmer for 2 hours or until amount of fluid is reduced by half. Strain carefully to reserve only the clear liquid. It is recommended for use in the fish soup on page 70, and can be used instead of clam juice in the chowder recipe on page 67.

Court Bouillon

2 quarts water
1 c. dry white wine
tbl. salt
sprigs parsley
1 small bay leaf
several peppercorns
1/2 tsp. dried thyme
2 stalks celery, ribs with 1 leaf, sliced in 2, 3 or 4 pieces
1 small carrot, coarsely chopped

This is a good, simple broth in which to cook shellfish, or poach fish such as bass and snapper, which will then be sauced.

Combine all ingredients in a 6-quart enameled or stainless steel pot and bring to a boil over high heat. Partially cover the pot, reduce heat, and simmer for 30 minutes. Strain through a large, fine sieve, and cool.

A traditional Greek table will include capers, the Mediterranean flower buds pickled in white wine vinegar. When buying them, always try to get the small imported ones. Some of the larger ones on the market today actually are nasturtium buds.

Capt. Anderson's

Baseball Hall of Fame hero Ted Williams
chats with Jimmy Patronis
on Thursday night, April 13, 1961.
Ted's choice that night? Baked Red Snapper.

Cocktail or Red Sauce and Seafood Seasoning

To 1 cup of ketchup or chili sauce, add 1 full teaspoon of prepared horseradish, a squirt of lemon juice and a couple drops of Tabasco. Simple, but the best.

For a seafood seasoning that is used at Captain Anderson's and one you can make yourself :

1/4 c. of salt (plain)	1 tbl. thyme
1/4 c. fresh ground black pepper	2 tbls. oregano
1/8 c. powdered garlic	1/2 tsp. cayenne pepper
1 tsp. sweet basil	1/4 c. paprika

Combine the ingredients and mix well. Store in a tightly sealed glass jar.

Garlic Butter

To 1/2 cup (one stick) well softened butter add the juice of 1 clove of garlic (use your garlic press). Add a pinch of salt. To the garlic butter, the addition of Parmesan cheese adds a nice touch for use on garlic bread.

Sauce Bercy

1 tbsp. finely chopped shallot	2 tbls. butter
3 tbls. white wine	1 tsp. finely chopped parsley
1 c. Fish Velouté	

Stew the shallot in the wine until the liquid is reduced by half, then stir into the veloute. Swirl in the butter and blend in the parsley. Makes about 1 1/2 cups. Serve with braised and broiled fish. Especially wonderful with fresh salmon.

Bouquet Garni is the traditional culinary posey, or nosegay. It has three common aromatic herbs, generally tied in a bundle or in a cheesecloth sack. They are parsley, thyme, and bay leaves. Many chefs add the bundle to sauces, casseroles, stews, and soups, removing it before serving. The proportions of the three main ingredients change according to the dish involved. In special cases, a bouquet garni may contain rosemary or lemon thyme or tarragon.

Capt. Anderson's

Jimmy Jr.'s Honey Dijon

1 1/2 c. mayonnaise
1 tbl. dry mustard
6 tbls. buttermilk
1/4 tbl. Lawry's Seasoning Salt
2 tbls. white wine
1/2 c. clove honey
1/2 tsp. poppy seeds
tsp. each black pepper, sugar,
1/4 tsp. Italian seasoning, cinnamon,
  paprika, allspice
2 cloves fresh garlic
1/4 c. chopped pecans

Jimmy Jr. (R) and Vasco Floyd, who has been with us since August, 1973.

Mix white wine and dry mustard and set aside. Mix all dry ingredients with honey and buttermilk until smooth. Fold in mayonnaise, then mustard paste. For best results, refrigerate for several hours. May be served as either cold or warm salad dressing.

Blender Hollandaise

1 1/2 c. (3 sticks) unsalted butter
4 egg yolks
2 tbls. water
dash salt

dash freshly ground white pepper
dash cayenne
1 1/2 tsps. lemon juice,
  strained

Melt butter over low heat until bubbling, but not brown.

Place all the remaining ingredients in the container of the electric blender. Cover; turn motor to high; at once remove cover and add the hot butter in a slow, steady stream. When all the butter has been added, turn off motor. Good as this recipe may be, it does not match the classic recipe.

To salvage Hollandaise (either blender or classic), that has not thickened properly or has curdled: place 1 teaspoon of lemon juice and 1 tablespoon of the sauce in a bowl that has been rinsed out in hot water and dried. Beat with a wire whip until the sauce becomes creamy and thickens. Then, beat in the remainder of the sauce, about 1 tablespoon at a time, whipping vigorously until creamy before adding next tablespoonful.

Leftover Hollandaise, tightly sealed in plastic wrap, can be refrigerated successfully for a few days, or it can be frozen. To heat: place in a pan of tepid (not hot) water until the right temperature has been reached. To thaw: take from the freezer a couple of hours before you plan to use it, then heat as directed. It is important to remember that Hollandaise is always served warm, never hot.

Makes about 1 3/4 cups sauce.

To make tempura batter, mix an egg and two cups of ice water. Beat until egg and water are blended. Add 3 cups of plain flour, a pinch of salt. Mix well. That is tempura.

Capt. Anderson's

Head Hostess Jean Brahier (L), and Crystel Sabochick. Jean has been with us since June, 1971, and Crystel has been with us since June, 1977.

Bechamel - White or Cream Sauce
(This makes a thin sauce)

1 tbl. unsalted butter
1 tbl. plain flour
salt and pepper

1 c. liquid (whole milk, light
cream or clam broth)

Melt butter and combine with flour in a small saucepan. Cook the two together until completely blended, stirring constantly. Stir in liquid with a wire whip until desired consistency is reached. If lumps appear, remove pan from heat and whisk the mixture until lumps are gone.

This sauce can be made thicker by adding extra tablespoons of both flour and butter while using the same amount of liquid as for the light sauce.

Today's nutrition-conscious hosts are serving more fish and seafood than ever before. Why? Because it's delicate in flavor and texture, light and easily digested, low in calories and cholesterol, and rich in fatty acids and trace minerals.

Capt. Anderson's

Oriental Steamed Rice

2 cups rice   1 teaspoon peanut oil
3 cups water

You must always use a heavy pot with a tight-fitting lid. No matter how much rice you're making, you must cover it with water to the exact depth of one knuckle on the slender finger of a pretty lady, which probably equals 3/4 of an inch. If you follow this fool-proof method, your rice will never fail. The proportions above are for 6 cooked cups.

Unless the package states otherwise, "wash the rice in seven waters" until the water runs clear; the washing gets rid of any protective talc the rice might have.

In a heavy pot with a tight lid, cover the rice with water to depth of one knuckle and add teaspoon of oil.

Bring rice to boil. When little "wells" begin to appear, set lid on firmly, turn heat very low, and steam for 15 minutes. Do not peek!

Remove pot from stove and, using chopsticks or a fork but never a spoon, gently fluff the rice from the bottom. Put lid back on and let sit for 5 minutes. In a heavy duty pot, rice will stay warm at least 30 minutes.

Rice made this way reheats well. Add 1 tablespoon of cold water to each cup of cooked rice and steam, tightly covered, for 8 minutes. The steam will fluff the rice perfectly. Steam by putting rice in a colander, over a pot of boiling water (be sure colander does not touch water). Cover the colander and steam for about thirty minutes until rice is fluffy.

Corn ground between steel rollers and stone ground corn is different. Southerners prefer stone ground, not for tradition but because it is better. Hulled corn with the germ removed is used to grind between steel rollers, which produce higher temperatures. Stone-ground cornmeal is ground at lower temperatures, which allows the entire kernel, with nothing removed, to be used. And the fat containing corn germ adds flavor to the meal.

Capt. Anderson's

Mornay Sauce

Prepare the basic bechamel sauce, using 1 cup of milk and 1 cup of fish stock for the required liquid. Add an additional 1/2 cup of stock to the sauce and reduce over a moderate heat to about 2 cups.

Over a very low flame, gradually add 1/2 cup of grated Swiss or Gruyere cheese, or a combination of grated Gruyere and Parmesan. Stir until the cheese is melted. Do not let this sauce boil after the cheese is added. Remove from the heat and swirl in 2 tablespoons of butter or margarine, one spoonful at a time. This will make about 2 cups of Mornay. If you want to make a Mornay Gratin for poached fillets, reduce the liquid in which fillets were poached until it is almost a glaze. Then add it to a basic Bechamel. Add 1/4 cup cheese and a tablespoon of butter as directed above. Spread over fillets and sprinkle with a few tablespoons of grated Parmesan. Then run it under the broiler. Be careful not to overcook.

A Rich Mornay Sauce

2 tbls. butter	6 tbls. Swiss cheese
2 tbls. plain flour	2 tbls. Parmesan cheese
1 c. whole milk	2 tbls. prepared mustard
1 c. Half and Half	white pepper
1 egg yolk	

Melt butter in shallow saucepan on medium heat. Add flour and blend completely. Add milk and Half and Half stirring constantly. Do not bring to boil. Slowly add one egg yolk; two for a very rich sauce. When thickened to desired consistency, add white pepper, mustard, chunks of the Swiss cheese and Parmesan cheese, until well melted and blended. Makes about 2 cups of a rich and tasty sauce.

Can be used on all manner of seafood, chicken, potatoes and other vegetables.

We put a blend on our "must have" list, but only brand-name Lawry's Seasoned Salt, no other. Lawry's is a superior blend and we use it extensively. It has no MSG. The essential ingredients include salt, sugar, paprika, turmeric, onion, cornstarch, and garlic. It's a nicely balanced time-saver for the serious cook.

Capt. Anderson's

How to Make Roux

Roux is a mixture of fat and flour, used to thicken sauces. It is essential to Creole and Acadian cooking. Roux is a French word that comes from the Latin "Russ," which means browned or reddish.

The more commonly accepted method of making Roux calls for equal parts of flour and a fat, which could be shortening, butter, margarine, oil, lard, or grease. This combination of fat and flour is stirred very slowly over a medium heat until a dark chocolate brown shade is reached. You'll have to be patient. It must be cooked very, very slowly or it will burn. One way to be safe is to turn down your heat when the color begins to match a brown paper bag. When you are ready to stop the browning process, just add your chopped vegetables, all at once. Next you add your liquid, either hot or cold.

Proportions and cooking methods can be varied with equally good results. Some cooks use only 1/3 to 1/2 as much fat as flour, claiming this blends more easily with the liquid without the danger of curdling. We have found that curdling often will take place when the process itself is rushed, so please take your time no matter what the proportions.

A less time-consuming method involves the oven. For this place 2 parts flour and 1 part fat in a flat pan and cook in preheated 275 oven for about 2 hours or until the roux has a rich caramel color. Stir every so often. Let cool, then drain off any excess fat.

For a batch of fat-free Roux, you'll want to cook in a 400-degree oven. Just use about an inch or so of flour. Stir often and cook until dark brown.

In any event, Roux can be made up in bulk ahead of time and refrigerated or frozen. It keeps well for a long time.

Garlic, perennial bulb of the onion family, probably is one of the best known herbs in the world, both as a food and as a medicine. The slaves who built the great pyramids got a ration every day in order to keep up their strength. Ditto the Roman soldiers. And in ancient Greece, garlic was seen as a symbol of strength and courage. Of course it's a "must have" item. You'll need it for just about every type of meal. Use sparingly, however, as it is strong and pungent. And here's a quick trick for a delicious treat that's really not too strong. Bake whole garlic heads for an hour at 300. Some folks like to brush them first with olive oil. They're good with or without. After they've cooled a bit, pull off clove and squeeze out the roasted garlic paste onto a cracker or a chunk of French, Italian, rye or pumpernickel. It can be a hit as an hors d'oeuvre, or alongside a main-course meat or vegetable.

Capt. Anderson's

James Warren, with us
since October, 1968.

Basic Crab Dip

8-oz. cream cheese
1/2 lb. crab meat
1-2 tbls. whole milk
2 tbls. fine chopped onion

1/2 tsp. prepared horseradish
salt to taste
fresh ground pepper

Mix to blend well. Bake about ten minutes at 375. Serve hot with crackers.

Crab Stuffed Mushrooms

20 large mushrooms, cleaned,
  and stemmed
1 egg beaten
2 tsps. onion, chopped
1/4 tsp. seafood seasoning
2 tbls. plain yogurt
2 tsps. finely chopped parsley

1 tsp. Worcestershire sauce
2 tbls. lemon juice
1/4 tsp. salt
1/2 lb. crab meat
Parmesan cheese and paprika
  as a topping

Arrange mushrooms in casserole or on large cookie sheet. Mix the rest of the ingredients and fold in the crab meat. Spoon a heaping amount into each mushroom cavity and sprinkle with cheese and paprika. Bake in preheated oven at 400 for 8 to 10 minutes.

There are two totally unrelated spices that we call pepper. They are the black peppercorn or pepperberry, and the large family that includes paprika, cayenne, and all the varieties of chilies identified as capsicums. Black peppercorns come from Malabar although the berries now are grown in other parts of the world. White pepper is the sun-dried pepperberry minus its pungent outer coating. It is less strong than the black. Green peppercorns are unripe berries that are packed in brine or wine vinegar. All of these peppercorns should, much like coffee, be stored in a cool place in a container with a tight lid. Your refrigerator or freezer would be fine.

Capt. Anderson's

Cheese Triangles
(Tyropittakia)

Filling I

3/4 lb. feta, crumbled
1/4 lb. Swiss
    cheese, grated
1/2 c. grated Parmesan cheese
1/2 lb. cream cheese
freshly ground pepper, to taste
grating of nutmeg, to taste

salt (optional, depending on
    saltiness of feta)
3 tbls. olive oil or butter
3 eggs beaten well
1 lb. commercial phyllo pastry,
    or 1 recipe, doubled, for any
    homemade phyllo dough
1 tbl. flour

Filling II

1 lb. feta, crumbled
1/4 lb. Parmesan
freshly ground pepper
1 lb. phyllo (see above)

2 tsps. dried mint
1/2 tsp. freshly grated nutmeg
3 tbls. olive oil or butter
3 eggs beaten well
1 tbl. flour

The traditional recipe is a simple combination of feta or mitzithra cheese, eggs, nutmeg, and sometimes mint. American Greeks use cream cheese in the filling, which is almost unheard of in Greece, and the use of several cheeses at once is a relatively new phenomenon. Also, the quantity of eggs may vary by one or two depending on the type and quality of feta used.

Tyropittakia are served piping hot as finger food and should be passed on a tray.

1. For either filling: Combine cheese, pepper, herbs and spices, olive oil or butter, and well-beaten eggs in a large bowl. Blend very well with a fork or wooden spoon. Refrigerate, covered, for at least 1 hour before using.

2. For packaged phyllo or strudel: Preheat oven to 350. Unroll phyllo and cut into thirds, lengthwise. Place a damp cloth over pastry to protect it from drying out. Remove one strip at a time. Brush with butter or olive oil. Fold right-hand side inward. Place 1 tsp. filling in middle bottom of strip. Fold right corner up and to the left, forming a right angle. Fold the strip upward at right angles until you reach the end, to form a small triangle. Place on cookie sheet. Repeat with remaining pastry and filling, for about 5 dozen. Bake for 20 minutes turning once, or until golden brown. Yield: About 5 dozen.

Pickled Shrimp

1 1/2 lbs. shrimp, raw	1/4 c. vinegar
1 pint beef stock	1 lb. thin onion slices
1/2 tsp. Tabasco	1 tbl. sugar
lemon slices	1/2 tsp. thyme

Combine all ingredients in a pot. Bring to a boil, reduce heat and simmer for about five minutes. Chill shrimp in the liquid. Drain and garnish with lemon slices and parsley.

Pickled Squid

2 lbs. squid	2/3 c. vinegar
2 tbls. olive oil or other oil	1/2 tsp. pickling spice
salt and pepper to taste	

Wash and clean squid. Steam in a covered pot for about 30 minutes. Drain and chop. Add remaining ingredients. Bring to boil, then simmer for 10 minutes or until tender. Chill and serve.

Greek Pickled Octopus

Cut the head off a large octopus and cube the meaty part. Cut the legs apart and steam all of it for about forty minutes, until slightly tender. Wash well with cold water and cut into bite sized pieces.

Place the octopus cubes into a glass fruit jar.

Mix together the following:

1 tablespoon of sugar	1/3 cup olive oil
1 tablespoon of oregano	2/3 cup of vinegar
2 cloves chopped garlic	1/3 cup of water
juice of one lemon	salt to taste

Stir until all ingredients are dissolved. Pour mixture over octopus making sure the octopus is completely covered. (More marinade may have to be made.) Put in the refrigerator for several weeks. The longer it remains in the refrigerator the more tender it gets. Serve cold.

Jimmy's oldest son, Theo circa 1963

Soups for All Seasons

It is unlikely any dish on the menu really can compete for international status as well as soup.

From places near and far come clear soups, vegetable soups, cream soups, chowders. There's Indonesian chicken and bean thread, Portuguese kale, German pea with sausages, Peking sour and peppery, West African yam . . . the list goes on and on. In this section we have included some regional favorites as well as some from the international menu. The French and Italian fish soups are wonderful.

Some fancy-pants once wrote that soup is to dinner what an overture is to an opera. Ain't so. Some soups really are the whole opera, and we've included examples, from hearty classic New England clam chowder (page 67) to Lee's filling gumbo (page 72). Try any one of them with some warm, fresh bread from our bakery and a good, fresh salad and you have a wonderful meal right there.

When cooking for low-cholesterol, low-triglyceride diets, you may freely use vinegar, spices, herbs, nonfat bouillon, mustard, Worcestershire sauce, soy sauce, and flavoring essences.

Capt. Anderson's

Egg and Lemon Chicken Soup
(Kotosoupa Avgolemono)

1 medium roasting chicken
1 large onion, unpeeled and studded
  with 2 cloves
2 to 2½ quarts water
salt to taste
freshly ground pepper

1 c. long-grain rice, bulgur, or
  trahana
3 eggs, at room temperature
strained fresh juice of 1 to
  2 large lemons

Bring chicken, onion, and water to a slow boil. Skim foam off top frequently. Add salt to taste and simmer, covered, for 2 to 3 hours, until chicken meat comes away from the bones. Turn off heat and remove chicken and onion from pot with a slotted spoon. Discard onion and debone chicken, shredding or chopping meat fine. Put chicken meat back in pot, bring to a boil, and add rice, bulgur, or trahana. Simmer, with cover ajar, until grain is cooked.

In a medium-size bowl beat together eggs and lemon juice until frothy. Very slowly add 4 to 5 ladlefuls (2 to 3 cups) of hot soup to egg mixture, beating vigorously with a whisk to keep egg from curdling. Pour egg mixture into pot and stir well with a wooden spoon. Serve immediately. Season individual bowls with freshly ground black pepper. Yield: 6 to 8 servings.

Paprika comes from the Hungarian word for pepper. Paprika is the powdered dry meat of the capsicum pepper, a distant relative of the ripe bell pepper. Sweet, delicate in flavor, it is quite the opposite of the chile or hot pepper. Paprika varieties include Hungarian and Spanish. Spanish is a bit stronger. Color ranges from bright red to light brown. The brighter the color the fresher. Paprika is sensitive to light. It is most often packed in tins. Store paprika in the refrigerator. It will keep for a year or more.

Capt. Anderson's

Bouillabaisse

2 1 1/2 lb. lobsters
1 qt. mussels
2 dozen medium clams
3 c. fish stock or water
splash of Tabasco
3 tbls. olive oil
2 leeks, white part only,
 finely chopped
1 1/2 tsp. thyme
1 large bay leaf
1 tsp. saffron threads, crushed
1/4 lb. butter

2 lbs. fresh striped bass,
 red snapper or sea bass
 cut into serving-size pieces
1 c. dry white wine
1 tbl. Pernod
1 onions, chopped
3 cloves garlic, minced
3 large tomatoes, peeled,
 cored and chopped
2 sprigs fresh parsley
1 1/2 tsp. flour

In large skillet, cook garlic, onions and leeks in olive oil until wilted. Add tomatoes, thyme, bay leaf, parsley, wine, water or the fish stock for a richer soup, saffron, and Tabasco. Simmer 10 to 15 minutes.

Prepare lobsters by separating tail from carcass. Cut tail into four round pieces, leaving the shell on. Split the carcass in half lengthwise and remove liver and coral. Blend them with butter and flour and set aside. Remove the tough sac near the eyes and discard. Break off the claws. Add the carcass to the skillet and cook, covered, for 30 minutes. Remove lobster and set aside.

Strain the tomato mixture through a medium sieve, pushing through as much of the solids as possible. Pour the broth into a deep pot and bring to a boil. Add the fish, mussels, clams, lobster pieces and claws. Cover and reduce heat to simmer for 15 minutes, or until mussels and clams open. Stir in butter mixture and bring to a boil. Turn off heat. Add Pernod and serve immediately. Yield: 5 to 6 portions.

Tabasco sauce — There are dozens of hot sauces with red or green peppers in a vinegar base. None compares to McIlhenny Company's Tabasco for elegance and refinement. Very simply, Tabasco is the best. It is a patented formula made from aged Louisiana peppers, light vinegar, and salt. We use it so often and in so many ways that it joins our "must have" short list.

Capt. Anderson's

Clam Chowder

Clam chowder, Manhattan or New England, is not often the soup du jour on the family menu in the South. But it could be. Clams are now harvested along the Gulf. Larger and somewhat stronger than the "little necks" of the Eastern shore, they are excellent in soups and stews.

New England Clam Chowder

2 c. cooked, diced potatoes
3 strips bacon, cooked crisp
1/2 c. minced onion
1/2 stick unsalted butter
1 tbl. Worcestershire sauce
1/3 c. flour

1 quart whole milk
1/2 c. half and half
3 8-oz. cans of clams
   or equal amount of fresh clams
   with the juice

Sauté onions in bacon drippings, crumble bacon, and add clams with broth and simmer for three or four minutes. In a four-quart sauce melt butter, blend in flour and add milk. Cook over medium heat stirring constantly, until mixture thickens. Reduce heat and add potatoes, clam mixture, bacon bits, Worcestershire sauce, salt and pepper to taste. Then add half and half, slowly. Do not let mixture boil.

In the language of food, beef, chicken and fish stocks are often referred to as Les Fonds de Cuisine, or the foundations of cooking.

Capt. Anderson's

Shrimp Creole

2 tbls. cooking oil
1/2 c. fine chopped onion
1/2 c. fine chopped celery
2 c. cooked, peeled, deveined
  shrimp

2 tsps. flour
1/4 tsp. fresh ground pepper
4 tsps. chili powder
1 16-oz. can tomatoes
1 tsp. Worcestershire sauce

Sauté onions and celery in oil until quite tender. Stir in flour, pepper, salt and Worcestershire. Add chili and tomatoes; simmer about 15 minutes and then add shrimp. Serve over rice.

Bay leaves, fresh garlic, oregano, thyme, brand-name McIlhenny's Tabasco pepper sauce, and brand-name Lawry's Seasoning Salt. To this add olive oil. That's because above all the other types, only the oil of olives produces the truly unique taste that our senior chefs demand. So there you have it. Our six-plus-one "must have" short list.

Capt. Anderson's

Charleston She-Crab Soup

1 tbl. butter
2-3 drops onion juice or a
little grated onion
2 c. crab meat and coral
eggs (crab roe)
3 1/2 c. whole milk
1 tsp. Worcestershire sauce

1 tbl. flour
1/2 tsp. MSG or Accent
dash of nutmeg
salt and black pepper to taste
6 tbls. sherry

Put butter, onion, crab meat and eggs in top of double boiler. Simmer for 5 minutes, combine 1/4 cup milk, Worcestershire sauce, flour, nutmeg, salt, and pepper. Stir until well blended into 1/4 cup cold milk. Heat remaining milk and combine with flour-milk mixture. Add to crab and cook slowly, 30 minutes. Pour into bowls, adding 1 tablespoon sherry to each bowl. If no coral eggs are available, grate yolks of 2 hard boiled eggs and add two spoonfuls to each bowl.

Crab Bisque

1/2 pound crab meat
1 1/2 tablespoons butter
3 cups Half and Half
1/2 cup whipping cream
1 1/2 tablespoons plain flour

2 tablespoons celery, diced
2 tablespoons dry sherry
paprika
dash of salt

Melt butter in a saucepan, blend in flour and cook until bubbly. Gradually, stir in Half and Half. Cook over low heat, stirring constantly until slightly thickened.

Add whipping cream, celery, crab meat, salt, pepper and sherry. Heat thoroughly, stirring often. Garnish with paprika.

Many definitions have been offered to separate spices from herbs. They both are vegetable products, used to add flavor and interest to cooking. Spices generally come from climates that are warmer than those where herbs grow. And since ancient times herbs have been cultivated for culinary as well as medicinal purposes. In fact, long before man kept records, he was using herbs for both food and medicine.

Capt. Anderson's

New Orleans' Style Fish Soup
(ersatz Bouillabaisse)

head and bones, red snapper or red fish preferred	3 bay leaves
1 1/2 quarts water	1 tsp. fresh thyme, minced finely (or 1/2 tsp. dried)
1/2 lemon, cut in very thin slices	1/2 tsp. salt
3 tbls. parsley, minced finely	1/2 tsp. pepper

. . .

4 lbs. fish fillets	4 c. tomatoes, fresh or canned Italian plum, chopped
salt and pepper, to taste	1 pint fish stock
3-4 cloves garlic, minced finely	salt, pepper, cayenne to taste
fresh thyme, minced finely (or dried)	1 lb. raw shrimp, peeled
allspice	pinch saffron
olive oil	buttered toast or fluffy rice (for 8-10 people)
3-4 onions, sliced	
2/3 c. sherry	

To make the stock, boil the head and fish bones in 1 1/2 quarts of water containing 1/2 lemon and parsley, bay leaf, thyme, 1/2 teaspoon of salt, 1/2 teaspoon of pepper. When the stock is reduced to one pint, remove the head and bones; strain the stock and reserve.

Rub each slice of the fish with salt and pepper and then with a mixture of garlic, thyme and allspice. Use a heavy hand here. Pour enough olive oil into a large pan to cover the entire pan.

Heat oil and add the sliced onion rings so they cover bottom of pan. Lay the fillets skin side up over the onions. Cover and simmer over a low-medium heat for about 10 minutes, turning once so that each side may be partially cooked. (The fish will be tender and may break.)

Remove fish and pour off any excess oil. Add the sherry and stir well. Add the tomatoes and the fish stock. Season to taste with salt, pepper, and cayenne.

(Continued on page 71)

Thymes, sage, mints, and marjorams grew in Biblical Times, along with hyssop and rosemary. From Egypt came coriander and cumin. And from India came anise, caraway, fenugreek, opium, thyme, and saffron. Herbs, spices, and aromatic oils were in great demand for medicines, cosmetics, perfumes, dyes, and disinfectants. And when the great pyramids of Egypt were being built, slaves were given garlic to keep up their strength.

Capt. Anderson's

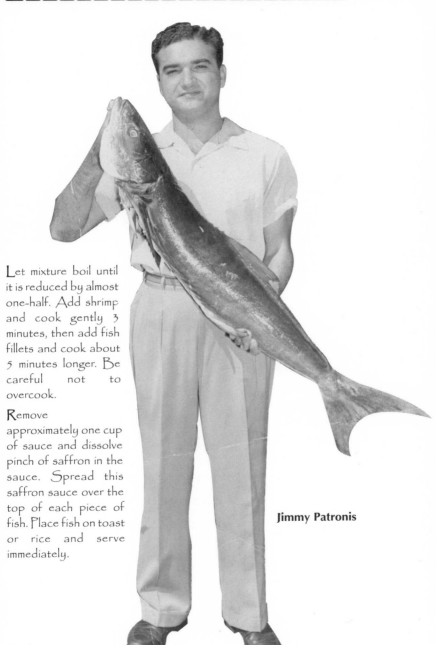

Let mixture boil until it is reduced by almost one-half. Add shrimp and cook gently 3 minutes, then add fish fillets and cook about 5 minutes longer. Be careful not to overcook.

Remove approximately one cup of sauce and dissolve pinch of saffron in the sauce. Spread this saffron sauce over the top of each piece of fish. Place fish on toast or rice and serve immediately.

Jimmy Patronis

Lee's Gumbo

1/2 c. oil
1 c. flour
4 quarts cold water
1 to 1 1/2 lbs. raw shrimp,
  peeled
1 pint raw oysters, washed
  and cleaned
1/2 lb. mild, smoked pork
  sausage, cut into
  bite-sized pieces
8 oz. okra, chopped (see
  options below)
2 large onions, finely chopped

1 large clove fresh garlic, minced
1 c. green onions and
  tops, chopped
1/4 c. parsley, finely chopped
1 medium bell pepper, chopped
2 ribs celery, chopped
1 bay leaf
1 splash Worcestershire sauce
1 tight pinch cayenne pepper
Tabasco. For the meek, drip to
  taste; for the hearty, splash to taste
2 pinches sea salt
1/2 tsp. fresh ground
  black pepper
1/2 tsp. filé (see options below)
cooked rice

In large pot, make roux with oil and flour. Cook over medium to low heat, constantly stirring until roux is dark enough — caramel to dark chocolate. Do not burn. (Recipe and tips for making roux are on page 58.) Remove from fire and add remaining ingredients, excepting the green onions, filé, rice, shrimp, and oysters. Return to fire, bring to boil, then reduce heat and very slow boil or simmer for 2 hours.

In the last 10 minutes add the green onions and shrimp. Keep at simmer, not a boil. For the final five minutes, add the oysters, cover and turn off the heat.

Serve six over hot rice in gumbo or soup bowls. Nice to have warmed French bread on the side.

Editor's Note: That wonderful, fine-ground greenish powder from sassafras

(Continued on page 73)

The red-hot regional cooking of Southern Louisiana reflects the influences of French, Native American, Spanish, and West African cooks. The name "gumbo" derives from a West African word for okra, a vegetable that traveled to the New World aboard slave ships.

Capt. Anderson's

circa 1969

leaves, which we call filé, serves as a thickener. So does the vegetable okra. Okra was introduced by African slaves and the Bantu word for it is ngombo. The Choctaw Indians introduced sassafras, which they called kombo. So the origin of gumbo remains in question. If you opt to use the okra, be exceedingly careful to use the filé only sparingly, otherwise the soup will become slimy. If you leave out the okra, the filé as a thickener may be added at the very last minute before serving, or at the table to taste. And that's the true nature of Gombo a la Creole, or Louisiana gumbo: it's a true blend of just about anything and everything, to personal taste. Gumbo technically means "all together" or "all at once," as in gumbo ya-ya, which means everybody talking all at once.

Please remember that fresh herbs and spices are much more pungent, and aromatic, than those that have been on the supermarket shelf. The difference fresh herbs make truly is dramatic. It is relatively easy to grow your own herbs. And fun. Even on a windowsill. We encourage it.

Capt. Anderson's

Italian Fish Soup
(Zuppa Di Pesce)

3/4 c. olive oil
2 cloves garlic, minced
1/3 c. shallots, minced
1 tsp. oregano
1 tsp. salt
pepper to taste
1/2-3/4 lb. striped bass fillet, skinned
1/2-3/4 lb. red snapper fillet, skinned
2 tbls. chopped parsley

8 medium shrimp, cleaned and deveined, tails on
1 squid, cleaned and cut in rings
10-12 sea scallops
1 c. dry white wine
8 littleneck clams, scrubbed
8 mussels, scrubbed and debearded
1 1/2 c. Italian plum tomatoes and their juice

Just the opposite of the classic French bouillabaisse, zuppa di pesce must be made quickly, preferably in a shallow vessel, and not allowed to boil. Making it is a quick procedure – assemble all the ingredients first.

Heat the olive oil in a large, heavy skillet with a cover. Add the garlic and shallots, cook until golden. Season with salt, pepper, and oregano, cook for 2 minutes longer.

Cut the bass and red snapper fillets into 6-8 pieces each and add to the olive oil mixture. Sauté the fish pieces until they just turn milky white, keeping them moving in the skillet, using a wooden spoon. Add the shrimp, sauté until pink, stirring frequently. Add the squid, scallops, and wine, bring just to boiling point, lowering heat immediately, and simmer for 2-3 minutes. Add the clams and mussels, cover the skillet with a tight-fitting lid, and cook for 10-15 minutes or until the clams open. Do not stir the contents at this time or the fish will come apart.

Break up the tomatoes lightly with a fork, add them to the skillet, and stir them in carefully so as not to break up the fish. Simmer, uncovered, until the sauce thickens, about 10 minutes. Correct the seasoning. Sprinkle with chopped parsley and serve at once. Serves 4.

If you are an apartment dweller without a windowsill, or an astronaut in a capsule on the way to Mars, or living in Newark, then you ought to buy those dried herbs in whole leaf form rather than pulverized. That way, you'll be able to crush what you need and it will give off a much more spirited and piquant taste. The same goes for spices. Buy them in whole form and grind as needed.

Capt. Anderson's

da State University head football coach Bobby Bowden flanked by brothers Yonnie (L) and Jimmy Jr. Both Patronis men are Florida State graduates.

Wendy's founder and owner Dave Thomas (L), joins Johnny Patronis (C) and Spanky McFarland of "The Little Rascals."

Jean Michel Cousteau (C), world-famous oceanographer, joins Yonnie (L), and Nick after a dive into one of Capt. Anderson's deep-sea dinners.

Classic Greek Salad
(Horiatiki Salata)

4 plump tomatoes, cored and
cut into eighths
1/3 lb. feta cheese, crumbled
1 tsp. dried oregano
1/4 c. olive oil
less, to taste
2 to 3 salted anchovies (optional)
15 to 20 kalamata olives

1 large red onion, cut
into thin round slices
1 cucumber, peeled and cut into
1/4-inch slices
2 green peppers, seeded and cut
into thin round slices
salt to taste

This is the classic Greek salad found on menus from Athens to Adelaide. Do it justice by choosing the best tomatoes you can find; sprinkle with sea salt, fleck with dried oregano, and drizzle into it some golden green olive oil. Combine tomatoes, cucumber, peppers, anchovies, olives, and half the onions and the feta in a medium-size bowl. Garnish with remaining onions and feta on top. Douse with olive oil and season with oregano and salt. Yield: 4 to 6 servings.

Store bought tomatoes (in winter) taste not too unlike the cartons they come in. This can be changed. First, do not refrigerate them. Place in a windowsill, where they will be decorative and the sun can shine on them, or place in a brown paper bag – unrefrigerated – and the flavor and texture will be greatly improved.

Capt. Anderson's

Lillian's
Tomato Greek Salad

The ingredients include a classic combination of tomato wedges, sliced cucumbers, black olives, and good-sized chunks of feta cheese. No lettuce, no celery. When the season and the mood are just right, it may have some rings of sweet Vidalia onion — as a harmonious ingredient and salute to our many friends from Georgia. This salad classic is drenched with olive oil, vinegar, and boasts a hint of fresh garlic.

Lillian (Mama) Lewis in our salad department is responsible for this long-time favorite.

Lillian Lewis - with us since December, 1953.

West Indies Crab Salad

2 lbs. cooked crab meat	4 tbls. lemon juice
2 small onions, chopped fine	1/2 c. white vinegar
Worcestershire	6 tbls. oil
fresh ground pepper, to taste	scant half c. of ice water

Spread a layer of crab meat and cover with a thin layer of chopped onions. Repeat until all crab and onions are used.

Mix vinegar, oil, lemon juice and Worcestershire. Pour over crab and onion mixture. Next, pour ice water along with some crushed ice over the entire surface until all is used. Add more ice water if needed to cover surface. Refrigerate overnight. Serve as appetizer or as an entree. Garnish with tomato wedges.

A Perfect Baked Potato

To bake a potato may seem to be a simple procedure. But to bake a perfect potato, there is more to it than tossing it in a hot oven.

First preheat oven to 400 to 425 degrees. Scrub potatoes under cold running water (Idaho bakers preferred). Choose potatoes of uniform size.

Dry the potatoes and with a fork pierce the skin at many points on the surface of the potato. This allows steam to escape and speeds baking.

Brush potatoes with olive or other oil, if you prefer soft skins after baking. A crisp skin is preferred today. The skin is a favorite part of the potato, among a growing number. Potato skins are now available as a snack food. Do not wrap in aluminum foil, if you desire a crisp skin.

Place potatoes directly on the oven rack and bake about an hour. Potatoes should feel soft when squeezed and can be easily pierced with a fork.

On removing the potatoes from the oven slash an X in the top of each potato. This allows the steam to escape and produces a mealy potato, not a soggy one. With a pot holder or towel squeeze the ends to help the steam escape, and the potato fluff. Mash with fork to fluff even more.

Our chefs encourage you to use herbs and spices more extensively in the preparation of your food, especially fish, soups, sauces, and salads. That's because herbs are at their best in light and wholesome foods, such as fish and salad. They are simply an excellent addition, for vitamins and healing properties, and without weight or richness.

Capt. Anderson's

University of Florida head football coach Steve Spurrier (L) with Nick.

Caesar Salad

4 or five slices French
or Italian bread
6 or 7 tbls. Virgin olive oil
1 head (large) Romaine lettuce
3 or 4 anchovy fillets
(rinse, dry and mince)
2 tbls. lime juice

1 clove minced garlic
1 tbl. dry mustard
1 tbl. Worcestershire
1/2 tsp. black pepper
1/2 c. Parmesan cheese
1 large egg

Brush one side of bread slices with olive oil. Toast in 400 degree oven until crisp and lightly browned. Repeat with other side of bread. Cut toasted bread into three-fourth inch cubes. Rinse and dry Romaine. Tear apart into two inch pieces. Mix the rest of the olive oil with the anchovies, Worcestershire, lime juice, garlic, mustard and pepper. Mix to blend thoroughly. Blend a warm soft boiled egg into above mixture. Add dressing, toasted bread cubes, and Parmesan to lettuce. Toss to coat Romaine evenly.

Some chefs like to use anise leaves with shellfish. Others put the seed in cakes, cookies, and breads. Anise is native to Egypt and popular throughout the entire Mediterranean. Its striking flavor resembles licorice. Old wives really know it's not a tale that a face pack made from ground aniseed will fade freckles.

Capt. Anderson's

Biscuits

2 c. all purpose flour
3 tsps. baking powder
3/4 tsp. sugar
1/4 tsp. salt

1/2 c. shortening
2/3 c. of whole milk
1/2 tsp. cream of tartar
(optional)

Mix dry ingredients with shortening and blend well. Add the milk and knead until well blended. Take a little extra time. On a sheet of wax paper or pastry board, roll a fourth of an inch thick on a well floured surface. Cut to size desired.

Bake on ungreased sheet until golden, not too brown. According to Executive Chef Alonzo Keys "you will have to hold the biscuits down to butter 'em."

Basil is wonderful with grilled fish. It also tickles the taste buds when added to tomatoes, eggs, mushrooms, and pasta dishes. It is rather common in French and Italian cooking. Basil has a strong flavor and should be used sparingly. The flavor increases when the leaves are cooked. There are two types of basil: sweet and bush. Both are annuals and the flavor is about the same for each.

Capt. Anderson's

Hush Puppies
(Makes 600-700)

Legend has it that hush puppies got their name many, many years ago when dogs gathered at the dining table along with everyone else. Licking their chops to get a morsel of food, they occasionally became noisy.

Cornbread was the usual bread served. It was often fried as are hush puppies today. Someone would toss a chunk of cornbread and say "hush puppy." It seems reasonable to say this is how the delicious companion to fish and seafood got its name.

20 lbs. plain flour	1 lb. salt
15 lbs. cornmeal (white)	2 lbs. baking powder
2 quarts eggs	8 lbs. onions, chopped
2 lbs. sugar	2 gallons buttermilk

In the Hobart mixer, mix first the dry ingredients. Add the eggs, onions and buttermilk. Mix to blend completely. Form into balls by machine, which automatically drops them into the deep fat cooker.

Hush Puppies - Family Recipe

1 c. white cornmeal	1/2 c. minced onion
3/4 c. plain flour	1 egg
2 tsps. baking powder	1/2 c. buttermilk
3/4 tsp. salt	3 tbls. cooking oil

Sift dry ingredients in a bowl. Add other ingredients and blend well. Shape into small balls with spoon or fingers. Fry in deep fat until golden brown. Drain well on paper towels or brown paper. Serves six people.

Rice pudding with a good, old-fashioned country secret. Store a couple of bay leaves in a jar of rice, or just add them to rice pudding. They'll beg for your recipe. And that's the story of bay laurel, which we also call sweet bay. It's a "must have" herb and one of the three in classic bouquet garni, the broth posey used to flavor good cooking. Some like to add a bay leaf to the broth when they poach fish. It has also been used in many marinades. Bay gives a spicy flavor to meats and vegetables, as well as soups and stews. Use it often.

Capt. Anderson's

Golden Cornbread

1 c. yellow cornmeal
1 c. flour (plain)
4 tsps. baking powder
1/2 tsp. salt

1 large egg, slightly beaten
1 c. whole milk
4 tbls. butter, melted
1/2 tsp. sugar

Sift dry ingredients into a bowl. Add the egg, milk and melted butter and mix thoroughly. Pour into a square baking pan with bottom only, greased. Put a few dabs of butter on top. Bake at 400 degrees in preheated oven for about twenty-five minutes. Set timer for twenty minutes and check. Should be golden brown.

Black-Eyed Peas

More than just eating ecstasy, black-eyed peas also are a symbol of good fortune. A Southerner, with just a glimmer of tradition, wouldn't think of ushering in the New Year without black-eyed peas cooked with hog jowl.

To cook these sublime pellets of the earth is an easy procedure.

2 c. dried black-eyed peas
10 c. hot water
a generous chunk of hog jowl
or ham hock

4 tbls. minced onion
1 1/2 tsps. salt

Carefully pick over the peas to remove anything that doesn't look as robust as it should. Put the peas gently in a large kettle of hot water. Add the salt, hog jowl and minced onion after water comes to a rolling boil.

Bring back to a boil, then reduce heat and simmer peas for about 2 1/2 hours, or until tender. Drain. Serve with cornbread. Enough peas for eight hungry people.

Borage gives a cucumber-type flavor to pea and bean soups. It is good with vegetable and green salads. In southern Europe, where it originated, borage was taken as a tonic to have an exhilarating effect on the mind.

Capt. Anderson's

Leon Harris and James Warren (foreground). James has been with us since October, 1968, and Leon came aboard in June of 1979.

CAPT. ANDERSON III
65 FT. DEEP SEA FISHING PARTY BOAT

Wonderful desserts are a trademark

The pièce de résistance is the dessert tray at Capt. Anderson's Restaurant. It is prepared in the excellent bakery where literally thousands of hard rolls, rye bread and other baked items are made daily. Capt. Anderson's always has fresh baked pies and cakes to "go home" with dinner guests.

Our dessert tray makes it difficult to decide and more difficult to turn down.

Number one on the popularity list is the feud cake. It was first served more than 40 years ago when the Patronis brothers operated the Seven Seas Restaurant in downtown Panama City. The recipe for this wonderful cake may be found on page 89. And we hope you'll enjoy the letter about it on page 88 just as much as we did.

Other items on the dessert tray include cheesecake, baklava (a Greek delicacy), lemon pie, coconut cream pie, silk and satin chocolate pie, and pecan pie. It also includes key lime pie and, frequently, a rich apple, or peach pie when fresh mouth-watering Georgia peaches are in season.

So please don't forget to visit our gift shop and take home some of our wonderful pastries and breads. We know you'll enjoy them.

Capt. Anderson's

Pastry Chef Tom Lannan, with us since April, 1995.

New York Cheesecake
with Fresh Strawberry Glaze

Cheesecake with the bright red cherry glaze is one of the favorites on our dessert tray. Don't forget to take some home from our gift shop.

4 8-oz. packages Philadelphia
   cream cheese (softened)
4 eggs
1 pt. sour cream

1 1/4 c. white sugar
3 tsp. cornstarch
2 1/2 tsp. vanilla extract

Beat cream cheese, sour cream and sugar until well blended. Add the eggs one at a time. Next add the cornstarch and vanilla and beat until smooth. Pour the mixture into a nine-inch spring form pan in which a layer of graham cracker crust has been placed on the bottom.

To make the crust . . . to a scant 2 cups of graham cracker crumbs, add 1/4 cup of sugar and 1/2 stick softened unsalted butter. Mix together until it forms a sticky mixture and press into the bottom of the buttered pan.

Bake the cheesecake mixture one hour at 350 to 375 in preheated oven. Turn off the oven and with the door open, let the cake remain for another hour. When cooled, refrigerate a few hours before releasing the pan from the cake.

To Make the Glaze

16 oz. fresh strawberries
1/4 c. sugar

1 tbl. cornstarch
1 tbl. lemon juice
2 drops red food color

Soak strawberries in splash of sugar water for hour or longer. In a small saucepan, combine the sugar and cornstarch adding the sugar water. Stir until mixture is smooth. Bring to a boil over medium heat, stirring constantly for a couple of minutes. The mixture should be thick and translucent. Remove from the heat and allow the mixture to cool slightly. Add lemon juice, and strawberries. Allow the glaze to cool completely and spoon over the top of the cool cheesecake.

Almond Florentine Cups

1/2 c. flour
dash salt
1/3 c. firmly packed brown sugar
1 egg, well beaten
1/2 c. toasted almonds
2 squares semi-sweet chocolate

1/4 tsp. baking soda
1/4 c. butter
2 tbls. light corn syrup
1/2 c. flaked coconut
1/2 tsp. vanilla
1 tbl. butter

Mix flour, soda, and salt. Cream butter. Gradually add sugar and beat until light and fluffy. Add corn syrup and egg. Blend well. Stir in flour mixture, coconut, almonds, and vanilla.

Onto greased baking sheets, drop by half teaspoonsful, leaving 2 inches between. Bake at 350 for 10 minutes. Cool on baking sheets for 1 minute, then remove quickly and finish cooling on racks. (If wafers harden on sheets, return briefly to oven.)

Melt chocolate and 1 tablespoon butter in saucepan over very low heat, stirring constantly until smooth. Drizzle over wafers. Yield: four dozen.

Chocolate Mousse Filling for Florentine Cups

1 1/2 tbls. sugar
1/4 c. water
2/3 c. sugar
1/4 c. dark rum

8 squares semi-sweet chocolate
8 eggs, separated
1 1/2 tsp. vanilla

Sprinkle 1 1/2 tablespoons sugar evenly on bottom and sides of well-buttered 9-inch pie pan. Melt chocolate in water in saucepan over very low heat, stirring constantly until smooth. Remove from head. Beat egg yolks and gradually add 2/3 cup sugar and continue beating until yolks are thick and light in color. Blend in chocolate, vanilla, and rum extract.

Beat egg whites and salt until mixture forms stiff peaks. Fold carefully into chocolate mixture, blending well. Measure 4 cups into prepared pie pan. Bake at 350 for 25 minutes, or until puffed and firm. Cool for 15 minutes; then chill for 1 hour. Spoon into chilled shell. Chill at least 3 hours. Before serving, garnish with sweetened whipped cream and/or chocolate-dipped fruit.

Recipe
on page 89

The Courier-Journal
The Louisville Times

525 WEST BROADWAY
LOUISVILLE, KENTUCKY 40202
AREA CODE 502-582-4011

May 19, 1987

Jimmy, Thanks ever so much for
the Cookbook - certainly have
enjoyed it.
         The cake has been quite
a hit - I can tell when people
are reading me by the number
of calls I receive when they
think I've goofed - the
2½ tablespoons of flour caused
quite a stir! The telephone
was wild.
         If I am ever in your area,
I'll be by to see you.
                    Sincerely,
                    Alice Colombo

P.S. Thanks again.

Captain Anderson's Famous Feud Cake

(Please note letter on page 88)

3 c. fine ground pecans
6 eggs, separated
1 1/2 c. granulated sugar

2 1/2 tbls. plain flour
1 tsp. baking powder

Beat egg yolks (by hand) for fifteen minutes adding sugar gradually. Add flour and baking powder, sifted. Add the pecan meal. Beat egg whites until stiff. Fold in.

Bake in two layers in a moderate oven, preheated to 350 degrees for thirty minutes.

Put layers together with 1 pint of whipped cream, sweetened and flavored with vanilla extract. Pile thick between layers, on sides and top. Sprinkle with ground pecans.

Key Lime Pie

1 can Eagle condensed milk
6-oz. lime jiuce
1 tbl. sugar

1 small container Cool Whip
1 graham cracker crust

This pie can be made quickly. A substitute for Key lime pie, which to be authentic would have to be made with limes coming from the Florida Keys.

Using packaged pie shells from the supermarket, save time, trouble and probably money. (Use plain or graham cracker.)

Back to the lime pie. Combine Eagle condensed milk, lime juice, sugar, and Cool Whip. Fold mixture until well blended. Pour mixture into graham cracker crust.

Chill. Garnish with more whipped topping or whipping cream. Add a few slices of fresh lime to garnish.

United States Senator Bob Graham (L) has been a long-time friend of the Patronis brothers. He's seen here with Jimmy Patronis during one of his visits to Capt. Anderson's Restaurant.

Coconut Pie

6 tbls. unsalted butter
3 eggs, large
1/4 c. buttermilk
1 c. sugar

6 oz. coconut,
(frozen or canned)
pinch of salt
1 tsp. vanilla extract

Beat eggs and add sugar and buttermilk. To this add melted butter and coconut. Add vanilla and salt. Bake in uncooked pie crust in preheated 350 degree oven for about ten minutes. Reduce heat to 300 degrees and bake another thirty-five minutes. Check for doneness.

Cayenne pepper always comes as a powder and it is made from various hot, dried peppers. It ranges from deep orange to fire-engine red. Cayenne supplies little savor but immense heat. You can use it sparingly in chicken salad, potato salad, cole slaw, and the like to give a bit of zing without changing flavors.

Capt. Anderson's

Sweet Potato Pie

1 1/2 c. boiled sweet potatoes	1/4 tsp. nutmeg
(peel, beat with mixer until smooth)	1/8 tsp. salt
1 c. light brown sugar	2 large eggs
1 tsp. powdered cloves	11/2 c. evaporated milk
1 tsp. cinnamon	

Blend spices, sugar and salt. Beat eggs with milk and combine with sugar spices and sweet potatoes until smooth. In saucepan, heat mixture until about to boil and pour into unbaked pie shell.

Bake in preheated 400 degree oven for ten minutes. Reduce heat to 350 degrees and continue to bake until knife comes out clean; about 30 to 40 minutes. Serve with whipped topping or whipped cream.

Lemon Meringue Pie

baked pie shell (9-inch)	1/4 c. lemon juice
1 c. boiling water	(Realemon can be used)
1/8 tsp. salt	3 egg yolks, slightly beaten
1 c. sugar	1 tbsp. or more unsalted butter
3 tbls. cornstarch	

Mix sugar, cornstarch and boiling water. Add egg yolks, lemon juice, butter and salt. Cook in double boiler until thickened. Cool, pour into baked pie shell. Top with meringue, whipped topping or whipped cream. If meringue is used, return pie to oven to brown the meringue.

Many know chamomile as an herbal hair rinse, others know it as a mouthwash. Some like it best when used as a soothing tea for an upset stomach or indigestion. Informatively, herbal teas are also called "infusions" or "tisanes." To prepare an infusion, warm a teapot but do not use a metal one. Add a tablespoon of dried herbs or a handful of fresh ones per cup. Steep for 10 minutes. Want a trick? Add herbs to ordinary tea for a pleasant surprise. Go ahead, experiment, be bold.

Capt. Anderson's

Zabaglione

1 pint fresh strawberries, washed and stemmed	1/2 c. sugar
8 egg yolks	2/3 c. Marsala or sweet sherry wine

A warm velvety custard, zabaglione is considered a great restorative in the Piedmont region of Italy, where it originated.

Divide strawberries among six stemmed wine glasses.

Put egg yolks, sugar and wine into round-bottomed copper pot or glass double-boiler top of at least 2-quart capacity, as egg yolks almost triple in volume. Sprinkle with cold water.

Place the copper or glass pot over a pan of simmering water and beat mixture rapidly with a wire whisk until it becomes a thick, creamy custard.

Immediately pour over the strawberries; serve at once.

If strawberries are not available, substitute sliced fresh, Georgia peaches, pitted fresh apricot halves, or sliced bananas.

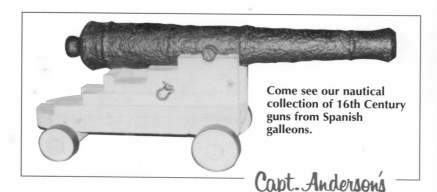

Come see our nautical collection of 16th Century guns from Spanish galleons.

Capt. Anderson's

Carrot Cake

4 large eggs	1 tsp. cinnamon
1 c. sugar	1 tsp. vanilla extract
1 1/2 c. corn oil	2 drops black walnut flavoring
1 c. carrots grated	2 c. self-rising flour

Combine eggs, sugar and oil. Add the rest of the ingredients. Mix well and bake in 10-inch tube pan which has been greased and floured. Bake in a preheated oven at 350 for 90 minutes. Check last 30 minutes. Do not over brown.

To ice cake . . . mix 1/2 box of powdered or confectioners sugar, 1 teaspoon vanilla extract and a few fine-chopped pecans. Add this to 8 oz. of cream cheese and 1/2 stick of softened butter. Spread over cooled cake.

Louisiana Pecan Pie

1/4 c. soft butter or margarine	1 tsp. vanilla
1 c. sugar	1 1/2 c. pecans
1 c. dark Karo syrup	salt
3 eggs	

Preheat oven to 350. With wooden spoon cream butter and sugar. Do not use an electric mixer. Add Karo and cream well. In separate bowl, beat eggs with whisk until they are light and lemon colored. Beat the eggs into the sugar mix. Add vanilla, pinch or so of salt to taste, and pecans.

Pour into unbaked 9" pie shell and bake at 350 for 45 minutes or until done. To test, insert knife halfway between edge and center of pie. If done, it should come out with a clear syrup coating.

Chili powder is a blend of ground dried chili peppers, garlic, oregano, cumin, and salt. There are a great variety of chili powders, ranging from relatively mild to call-out-the-fire-department. Supermarket chili powder usually has too much filler and too little character. So we suggest you buy a better quality in a Latin American, Caribbean, or Oriental market.

Capt. Anderson's

Flaky Pie Crust

4 1/2 c. unsifted all purpose flour   1 large egg
1 tablespoon sugar   1 tbl. white or cider vinegar
2 teaspoons salt   1/2 cup water
1 3/4 cups solid vegetable shortening
(no substitutions)

No matter how much you handle this dough, it will always be flaky and tender. It may be refrigerated for three days or it may be frozen until ready to use. This recipe will make 4 to 5 single crusts.

Put flour, sugar and salt in large bowl and mix well with fork. Add shortening and mix with fork until ingredients are crumbly. In small bowl, beat egg, vinegar and water. Combine the two mixtures, stirring with fork until all ingredients are moistened. Divide dough into five (5) portions. Wrap each in plastic wrap and chill for at least 1/2 hour.

Roll pie crust out between two pieces of plastic wrap. This makes job easier by eliminating need for extra flour. When crust is rolled to desired size, peel off top wrap. Invert into pie plate and peel off plastic bottom wrap.

For baked shell, prick bottom and sides of pastry thoroughly. To keep shell flat, place parchment paper or foil over crust. Press gently into the crust. This will help prevent shrinking. Put on rack in center of preheated 400 oven. Bake 10 minutes or until crust has set. Then remove foil or parchment and bake until brown for approximately 5 to 8 minutes.

Hint: Shiny metal pans reflect heat away from crust. For better browning of crust use dark metal or clear Pyrex pans.

Cinnamon is a must for most kitchens. It's very hard to grind so in this exception, buy it in powdered form. Produced from the bark of the cinnamon tree, this heady spice is a favorite in lamb dishes. It also lends a fragrance to cakes, cookies, pies, and sauces.

Capt. Anderson's

Silk and Satin Chocolate Pie

2 squares Hershey chocolate
(unsweetened and melted)
1 stick unsalted butter
3/4 c. of sugar
1 tsp. vanilla extract

2 large eggs, chilled
1 pie shell, baked and cooled
whipped cream or topping
slivered almonds, toasted

Cream butter and sugar until very light and fluffy. In double boiler, melt chocolate and blend with vanilla. Add the chilled eggs, one at a time. Beat with electric beater on medium speed at least two minutes after adding each egg.

Pour into baked pie shell. Chill at least three hours in refrigerator before serving. Top with whipped cream or whipped topping and toasted almond slivers. This is one of our dessert tray favorites.

Georgia Peach Cobbler

8 ripe Georgia peaches
1/4 tsp. cinnamon
1/2 c. of flour (plain)

1/2 c. of sugar
1/4 tsp. salt
1/2 stick unsalted butter

Grease a one-quart glass baking dish. Peel and slice the peaches. To easily peel a peach, place them in very hot water for ten or fifteen seconds and the peel will slide off. Place the peeled and cut peaches into the bottom of the baking dish. Mix flour, sugar, cinnamon and salt. Cut in the butter to completely blend.

Spoon this mixture over the peaches and press down evenly. Make a couple of holes in this mixture, which will become the crust. Bake at 400 degrees for twenty to twenty-five minutes. Check occasionally.

Chives are used in many dishes, from salads to vegetable soup, from baked potatoes to omelets. Because chives have a very mild onion flavor, they can be used in dozens of recipes where subtlety is favored.

Capt. Anderson's

Crepes

1 c. flour
1 whole egg
1 egg yolk
1 1/2 tsps. sugar

2 tbls. melted unsalted
    butter or margarine
1 tsp. vanilla extract
1 1/4 to 1 1/2 c. milk

Put flour in a bowl. Slowly add the egg and the egg yolk while stirring with a wire whisk. Add a half cup of milk. Beat to make the mixture as smooth as possible. Add more milk to make the batter the consistency of heavy cream. Stir in the sugar, butter or margarine, and vanilla. If you use a beater, you must let the batter stand for at least 2 hours.

To cook the crepes, rub the bottom of the crepe pan with a piece of paper toweling that has been dipped in butter or margarine. This is necessary for the first crepe and probably unnecessary after the first crepe has been made if pan is properly cured.

Throw the first crepe away. Now you're really ready. Depending on size of pan, spoon 2 to 4 tablespoons of batter into pan and quickly swirl until bottom is evenly coated.

Crepe should be quite thin. Cook briefly until crepe "sets" and starts to brown lightly on bottom. Using a spatula, turn crepe and cook briefly on other side without browning. Turn out onto waxed paper. Remember that when a crepe is properly made you can see through it when held up to the light.

Yields about a dozen.

Spicy cloves are the unopened buds of the clove tree. They have a powerful fragrance and are used in dishes ranging from beef casseroles to cookies.
Please remember that just a few go a long way.

Capt. Anderson's

Classic Baklava

1 lb. unsalted butter	3 c. zwieback biscuit crumbs
2 lbs. commercial phyllo or	1/2 lb. margarine
strudel pastry	10 c. coarsely chopped walnuts
whole cloves (optional)	or blanched almonds, or
	mixture of both

Syrup:

4 c. sugar	2 tbls. strained
4 c. water	fresh lemon juice

Clarify butter and margarine: Place butter and margarine in a small saucepan and heat slowly over low heat. Remove pan from heat and cool for 2 to 3 minutes. With a spoon, skim the milky foam from the top of the butter and discard foam. Pour the remaining clarified butter in a bowl and set aside.

Preheat oven to 400. Lightly butter a 15 x 18 x 3 baking pan.

In a large bowl, combine nuts and zwieback. Add 1/4 to 1/3 cup clarified butter/margarine to the mixture; enough to moisten it.

Layer 6 phyllo sheets on bottom of prepared baking pan, one at a time, brushing each one generously with butter and margarine mixture. Sprinkle about a third of the nut mixture over the sixth phyllo sheet and spread it evenly. Drizzle 1 to 2 teaspoons more butter and margarine over nuts.

Layer 4 phyllo sheets over the nuts, one at a time, buttering each generously. Spread another third of the nut mixture on top and drizzle, as before, with a tsp. or two of butter and margarine. Layer and butter another 4 phyllo sheets, top with remaining nut mixture, and drizzle with clarified butter and margarine. Top the pan with 5 to 6 sheets of phyllo, each brushed generously with butter and margarine. With the tips of your fingers, sprinkle the top phyllo with a little water, and brush again. Score into diamond shapes, first cutting gently with a sharp knife vertically, then horizontally, making sure the knife cuts all the way

(Continued on page 98)

Coriander, an annual, is spicy and aromatic, and most common in Mediterranean cooking. The dry whole seed is used.

Capt. Anderson's

down through the very bottom phyllo. To make the tray more decorative, press a whole clove into each piece of baklava, if desired, before baking.

Bake for 10 to 12 minutes, or until the phyllo begins to crisp and brown slightly. Reduce heat to 325 and bake for 1 1/2 to 2 hours, or until golden brown. Five minutes before removing baking pan from oven, brush with one more ample dousing of butter and margarine.

To prepare syrup: In a large saucepan combine sugar and water and bring to a rapid boil. Reduce heat and simmer, uncovered, for 12 to 15 minutes, until syrup is thick. Remove from heat and immediately stir in lemon juice.

Pour hot syrup over the baklava. Place baklava in oven which has been turned off but is still hot and let stand until all the syrup is absorbed; about 20 minutes.

Serve warm or at room temperature. Yield is about 30 pieces.

Amaretto Cheese Cake

3 pkgs. dry gelatin	3/4 c. cold water
2 lbs. cream cheese	12 oz. sugar
1 small can condensed milk	1 tbl. lemon juice
1/2 c. graham cracker crumbs	2 tbls. Amaretto

Cream the cream cheese and sugar until smooth. Add milk and cream again. Separately, combine cold water and gelatin in small sauce pan. Milt over low heat. Stir. Add Amaretto and lemon juice to gelatin mix. Add mixture to cream cheese. Fold in the cream cheese mix into the gelatin mix.

Pour mixture into greased spring form pans that have been dusted with graham cracker crumbs. Yield: about 10 slices.

Used extensively in Mexican cooking, cumin is grown only for its seed, which is strongly aromatic and has a strong, warm taste. It also fits nicely into Mediterranean recipes.

Capt. Anderson's

Helen's Baklava

4 c. finely chopped nuts
1 lb. phyllo
1 1/2 c. melted butter

4 tbls. sugar
2 tsps. ground cinnamon

In a large bowl, mix nuts, sugar, and spices. Open and place defrosted phyllo on plastic covered working surface. Cover stacked phyllo with a towel to eliminate drying. Place a sheet of phyllo oblong on your working surface. Brush generously with melted butter. Place a second sheet of phyllo over the first, brush with butter. Repeat for a third and fourth time. Sprinkle 2/3 cup nut mixture over the phyllo.

Starting with the bottom edge roll loosely like a jelly roll, making a long roll. Place in a buttered baking pan. Continue making additional rolls until all mixture is used. Brush the tops of the rolls with more melted butter. Cut the rolls diagonally into 1 1/2 inch size pieces. Bake at 325 for 25 to 30 minutes.

The rolls should be a light gold. Set aside to cool in pan. Let stand at least an hour, or better yet, overnight.

Syrup:

3 c. sugar
1 1/2 c. water

juice of 1/2 lemon or lemon slices
2 tbls. pure honey

In a large saucepan combine the sugar, water and lemon. Simmer for ten minutes. Slowly stir in the honey and simmer for five minutes longer. Spoon warm syrup over cool baklava rolls. Let stand overnight.

Some Indian curry blends call for as many as 30 ingredients. These may include tumeric, coriander, cumin, ginger, black pepper, cardamon, fennel, red peppers, mace, cloves, yellow mustard, poppy, garlic, fenugreek, and cinnamon.

Capt. Anderson's

Nut Cake
(Ravanie)

14 eggs, separated	3 c. ground almonds
1 1/2 c. sugar	rum syrup
1 tsp. vanilla extract	16 pieces of ground zwieback
3 c. ground walnuts	grated rind of one orange

Preheat oven to 350. Grease 16 x 13 x 3 pan. Beat whites of eggs until stiff and set aside. Beat the yolks with sugar until light and lemon colored. Add vanilla to the yolks while beating. Mix the nuts, zwieback and rind together.

Gradually fold the beaten egg whites into the yolks and fold into the nut mixture. Pour batter into prepared pan and bake exactly one hour. While baking prepare the syrup by mixing over moderate heat:

2 c. sugar	1 slice lemon
4 c. water	1/2 c. light rum
1 stick cinnamon	

Pour the hot syrup over the cake the moment it is removed from the oven. Cool before serving. Cut into diamond shapes.

Dill makes a dilly of a sauce to go with fish. It's as if they were made for each other. Probably were. And this fragrant annual has lots of other culinary uses, too. You can use whole or ground dill seed in lamb stews, herbal butters, soups, salads, dressings. . . even pickles. If you're going to enjoy Middle Eastern recipes, you'll need dill in your kitchen.

Capt. Anderson's

Executive Chef Alonzo Keys (L) and Johnny Patronis. Alonzo has been with us since November, 1953.

Wedding Cookies
(Kourabiedes)

1 lb. sweet butter	1 tsp. baking powder
1/2 c. sugar	5 c. sifted cake flour
2 egg yolks	3 boxes confectioner
1-oz. whiskey	powder sugar
1 tsp. baking soda	1 c. chopped nuts

Cream butter and sugar. Add egg yolks, flavorings and beat until well blended.

Remove from beater and gradually add flour to the mixture. Must be a soft dough. Pinch off pieces of dough and shape into silver dollar size rounds. Place on greased cookie sheet one inch apart. Bake at 375 for about 20 minutes or until light tan. As cookies are removed from oven and while still hot, sift confectioner sugar over each cookie, covering it well. Makes 40 to 50 cookies.

Raw to Cooked

Rice, one cup equals 3 cups cooked

Noodles, 1 cup equals 1 1/2 cups cooked

1 pound of coffee equals 40-50 cups

Lemon equals 2-3 tablespoons juice

Orange equals 1/2 cup juice

1 pound loose tea equals 145 teacups

1 pound potatoes equals 2-3 cups mashed

Cream Heavy, 1/2 pint equals 2 cups whipped

Macaroni, 1 cup equals 2 cups cooked

Cheese, 1/4 pound equals 1 c. grated

Graham crackers, 11 crackers equals 1 cup crumbs

Fahrenheit Oven Temperatures

250 to 275 ....very low

300 to 325 ....slow

350 to 375 ....moderate

400 to 425 ....hot

450 to 475 ....very hot

500 to 525 ....extremely hot

Basic Measurements

3 teaspoons equals 1 tablespoon

2 tablespoons equals 1 ounce (or 1/8 cup)

4 tablespoons equals 1/4 cup

8 tablespoons equals 1/2 cup

16 tablespoons equals 1 cup

4 quarts equals 1 gallon

2 cups equals 1 pint

1 pint equals 16 ounces

1/2 pint equals 8 ounces

8 oz. equals 1 cup

4 cups equals 1 quart

1 quart equals 32 ounces

pound = lb. pounds = lbs. cup, cups = c.
ounce, ounces = oz. teaspoon = tsp. teaspoons = tsps. tablespoon = tbl.
tablespoons = tbls.

Capt. Anderson's

Index

(Continued on page 104)